INTEGRATED
COMPUTER PROJECTS

Maryanne Momorella
Business and Technology Teacher
Kintnersville, PA

Wendy Hohenstein
Technology Teacher
Kintnersville, PA

SOUTH-WESTERN
★
THOMSON LEARNING ™

Australia • Canada • Mexico • Singapore • Spain • United Kingdom • United States

SOUTH-WESTERN

™

THOMSON LEARNING

Integrated Computer Projects
Wendy Hohenstein, Maryanne Momorella

**Vice President/
Executive Publisher:**
Dave Shaut

Team Leader:
Karen Schmohe

Acquisitions Editor:
Jane Congdon

**Executive Marketing
Manager:**
Carol Volz

Channel Manager:
Nancy A. Long

Marketing Coordinator:
Cira Brown

Production Editor:
Todd McCoy

Consulting Editor:
Diana M. Trabel

Production Manager:
Patricia Boies

**Manufacturing
Coordinator:**
Charlene Taylor

Compositor:
Publishers' Design and
Production Services, Inc.

Printer:
Quebecor
Dubuque, IA

Design Project Manager:
Stacy Jenkins Shirley

Internal Designer:
Joseph R. Pagliaro

Cover Designer:
Joseph R. Pagliaro

Library of Congress
Cataloging-in-Publication
Data

Contents

Contents

Contents

Preface

We wrote this book because as teachers, we could not find an appropriate text to meet the needs of our computer applications students. We decided to write activities that would require our students to use application software to complete realistic and practical tasks. These 28 projects will give you more than 80 hours of engrossing, educational activities and projects to share with your classmates.

Features

- These projects have been field-tested and revised several times, so they're ready to use.

- They are designed as an integrated software approach that includes several software applications within each project.

- The core curriculum areas of language arts, mathematics, science, and social studies are integrated throughout the book.

- The computer skills correlate to the National Educational Technology Standards (NETS).

- The projects are generic; they can be used with any software package, as well as with PCs or Macintosh computers.

- The projects are not sequential; you can complete them in any order.

- Many of the projects encourage you to work with a partner or a team.

How This Book Is Organized

- The book is divided into four parts—basic, intermediate, advanced, and capstone project. The capstone project draws upon all the skills in the previous parts.

- This book is not intended to teach software applications. Instead it provides hours of reinforcement of software skills in a fun, practical environment.

- Problem-solving skills are used throughout the text. You are encouraged to create documents and use the software's Help feature to learn more advanced skills.

- Each part builds on previous skills and utilizes more advanced skills as you progress through the book.

- Core curriculum standards and computer competencies are highlighted in the skills charts found in the Teacher's Manual.

Project Learning Features

- Completion time estimate for the entire project in the Teacher's Manual and for each section in the student book.

- Core curriculum areas covered.

- Project objectives.

- A scenario that sets the theme for the project.

- Computer skills used.

- Each project is divided into sections to allow students to master small pieces of the project before moving on to the next section.

- Tips and Notes that help you as you work through the project.

- A scoring rubric checklist for you and your teacher to evaluate your work (in the Teacher's Manual).

- Curriculum Connections that offer fun optional activities to enhance your understanding of the computer skills emphasized in the main project. Each optional activity correlates to one of the four core curriculum areas of language arts, mathematics, social studies, and science.

Capstone Project

The final project, *The Case of the E-Mail Enigma*, is a fully integrated murder mystery. You will solve the case using word processing, databases, spreadsheets, desktop publishing, and presentation software. You'll have to read carefully to find all the clues to solve the mystery!

About the Authors

Wendy Hohenstein recently retired after 22 years teaching high school and middle school business and technology courses. She now teaches adult technology courses. She lives in Pennsylvania with her husband, Steve; two dogs; three horses; and three cats.

Maryanne Momorella has been teaching high school business subjects for 24 years. She currently teaches in the Business and Technology Department at Palisades High School in Kintnersville, Pennsylvania. In addition to her teaching, Maryanne has been an advisor to the Future Business Leaders of America for the past 22 years. She resides in Horsham, Pennsylvania. In her spare time she enjoys golf, horseback riding, spending time with family, friends, and her spunky dog, Kinsey.

Basic Projects

Project

1

Write-Around the Room!

As a member of the Journalism Club, you volunteered to obtain writing from a number of students in the school for publication in the school newspaper. You decide to use a write-around technique. The newspaper will end up with stories written by ten or more students, working as a team.

In this project you will:

- ☑ **Compose a story**
- ☑ **Insert footnotes**
- ☑ **Check spelling**
- ☑ **Edit your story**
- ☑ **Insert headers and footers**
- ☑ **Illustrate with graphics**

Project Curriculum Skills

Language Arts

Story Start

1. Choose a story start from the list provided by your teacher.

2. Type the story start using your word processing software.

3. Save the file.

4. After typing the start, start a new paragraph, and continue writing the story in your own words.

5. When you have typed a few sentences or more, insert a footnote containing your first and last name at the end of the paragraph.

SKILLS CHECK

If you need help with footnotes, use your software's Help feature and your word processor to write the steps for inserting footnotes.

NOTE

You may want to write more than a paragraph if you have a particular direction you wish to take with the story.

Write-Around

1. Now it's time to move to another student's computer.

2. Read what has been written so far.

3. Begin a new paragraph, and continue the story.

4. When you are ready to move to another computer, insert a footnote containing your name at the end of your paragraph.

5. Save the story.

6. Continue writing at different computers until your teacher tells you to stop.

Write an Ending

1. When you return to your computer, read all that has been written.

2. Compose an appropriate ending to the story.

3. Save the story again.

Edit Your Story

1. Spell check the story.

2. Edit your story.

   a. Read the story from start to finish.

   b. Be sure that the story makes sense.

   c. Make any changes necessary to make the story flow as if one person wrote it.

   d. Create a title for the story and place it at the top of page 1.

3. Insert headers and footers to begin on page 2.

   a. Header: Type your first and last name.

   b. Footer: Type the story title at the left and insert the page number at the right.

4. Illustrate your story with graphics. Use clip art graphics, if available, or create your own.

5. Apply formats such as bold and italic to the document to make it more attractive.

6. Save the story again.

SKILLS CHECK

If necessary, use your software's Help feature and your word processor to write the steps for inserting headers and footers.

NOTE

Formatting Suggestions for Word Processing Documents
- ✔ Use at least a 12-point font and an easy-to-read font style.
- ✔ Center and apply formatting to headings and titles when appropriate.
- ✔ Emphasize words and phrases by using bold, italic, or underline.
- ✔ Emphasize important information by using bullets or numbering.
- ✔ Insert clip art where appropriate.

Write-Around Story Starts

1. The thunder of hooves rang out across the desolate terrain. The horses were tired and hungry, but I had to keep pushing them. There was precious little water to be found, and we were sitting ducks for rustlers in this flat, open country.

2. Today was "family day" at the park. As Mom, Dad, and my little sister finished their picnic lunch, I wandered toward the edge of the woods. No one noticed as I followed a path deeper and deeper into the forest. Suddenly, the path ended at the opening to a dark cave. I stopped for a moment and then decided to explore. As I ducked into the opening, I noticed a strange smell.

3. It was summer vacation, and my friends and I had nothing to do. As we waited for my Mom to drive us to the pool, we decided to dig a hole in the flowerbed. Of course, we'd have to fill it in before Mom saw it, but we'd worry about that later. We dug deeper and deeper. Suddenly, a strange rumbling noise came from the hole.

4. It was an average day at Beverly Hills Middle School, where we were in computer class, gamely learning all about spreadsheets. Suddenly a bolt of lightning illuminated the lab, followed by a clap of thunder. The inevitable power surge crackled through the network, leaving all but Mrs. Gonzales' computer in a mass of melted plastic.

5. The pleasure of my daily run one chilly April morning was abruptly shattered by the shrill wail of a siren. I followed the sound along a narrow alley.

6. "One thousand one, one thousand two, one thousand three. . . ." The seconds seemed like hours as I struggled to focus on the math problem at hand. The clock made its painfully slow ascent toward 2:44, and finally, I was free. I shot down the hall toward the exit, dodging bodies as I thought about what was to come. Summer vacation was finally here!

7. The insistent ringing of the phone abruptly wrenched me from a sound sleep. The illuminated hands on the bedside clock read 2 a.m., an atrocious hour for anyone to call.

8. "I *will* make it. I *will* make it." The chant continued in my head as I marched through the main entrance of Columbia Records, Inc. The elevator walls were lined with pictures of my idols that seemed to mock me as they smiled down at my shaking knees and pounding heart. "Pull yourself together," I commanded myself as I stepped off the elevator.

9. Her eyes were green—as intense as the jungle that surrounded her. I watched the tiny shaft of sunlight dance on her golden hair. The cries of the jungle's inhabitants went unnoticed as our eyes met.

10. The scorching pain in my shoulder jolted me awake. The blood on my shirt confirmed that I had been wounded. As I dragged myself upright, I struggled to remember what had happened.

Curriculum Connection

Read the stories completed by your class. Do the stories contain any plots that remind you of current happenings in the news? What current events do they resemble?

National Sweepstakes

Congratulations! **You just** won the National Sweepstakes second prize—$120,000. It's not $10 million, but it sure is nice! You'll be receiving $10,000 on the first of each month for the next 12 months.

Create a spreadsheet that shows what you will buy each month. Add a sheet to the workbook to show what you will save toward your college fund.

What will you do with all this money? Be creative!

In this project you will:

☑ **Create a spreadsheet**

☑ **Use formulas**

☑ **Add a sheet to the workbook**

☑ **Rename the sheet**

☑ **Insert graphics in a workbook**

Project Curriculum Skills

Mathematics

Create the Spreadsheet

SKILLS CHECK

The Balance column will contain the formula to calculate the amount spent from the $10,000 deposit. If you're unsure about how to use formulas, use your software's Help feature and your word processor to write the steps for creating formulas.

1. Design your spreadsheet using the one shown in Figure 2-1 as a model.

2. Begin each month with a $10,000 deposit.

3. End each month with money left in the account. You'll put this money toward your college fund. The goal is to put most of the money in the college fund.

4. Continue adding items to the spreadsheet until you've completed 12 months of data. You must end up with at least $2,500 in your account at the end of each month.

5. Save the spreadsheet.

	A	B	C	D	E	F	G
1		GREGOR'S BANK RECORD					
2							
3	DATE	DESCRIPTION	DEPOSITS	EXPENSES	BALANCE		
4	9/1/2001	WINNINGS--FIRST MONTH	10000		10000		
5	9/4/2001	Snow skis for brother		500	9500		
6	9/7/2001	Snow skis for me		600	8900		
7	9/10/2001	Gift for teacher		5	8895		
8	9/13/2001	New TV for big sister		500	8395		
9	9/16/2001	Humane Society of US		1000	7395		
10	9/19/2001	One T-shirt for little brother		9	7386		
11	9/22/2001	New tools for mom and dad		350	7036		
12	9/25/2001	Motorized scooter		2500	4536	***to my college fund*	

Figure 2-1 Bank record

Calculate Your College Fund

SKILLS CHECK

If necessary, use your software's Help feature and your word processor to write the steps for naming a new sheet.

NOTE

Use the ending balance each month for the college fund amounts.

NOTE

Formatting Suggestions for Spreadsheets
- ✔ Use an easy-to-read font style and size.
- ✔ Distinguish column headings from data by using bold, italic, underline, and fill colors.
- ✔ Emphasize the title of the sheet by using larger font size or a color, or both.
- ✔ Format all dollar amounts to two decimal places and use the dollar sign.
- ✔ Insert clip art where appropriate.

1. In the same file, create a new sheet for your college fund.

2. Name the new sheet *College Fund*.

3. Rename Sheet 1 *Bank Record*.

4. Save the file.

5. List all the amounts you set aside for your college fund, as shown in Figure 2-2.

6. Apply formats such as bold, italic, and fill colors to the spreadsheet to make it attractive. You might also add appropriate clip art.

7. Save the file again.

	A	B	C	D
1	**Gregor's College Fund**			
2	**Date**	**Amount**	**Balance**	
3	1/25/02	$6,500	**$6,500**	
4	2/25/02	$5,500	**$12,000**	
5	3/25/02	$8,000	**$20,000**	
6	4/25/02	$7,899	**$27,899**	
7	5/25/02	$5,920	**$33,819**	
8	6/25/02	$6,950	**$40,769**	
9	7/25/02	$8,967	**$49,736**	
10	8/25/02	$7,500	**$57,236**	
11	9/25/02	$4,536	**$61,772**	
12	10/25/02	$7,890	**$69,662**	
13	11/25/02	$9,000	**$78,662**	
14	12/25/02	$5,500	**$84,162**	
15				
16				
17				

Bank Record \ **College Fund** / Sheet3

Figure 2-2   College fund

Curriculum Connection

Calculate how much you would have in your college fund if you received 5% interest. Calculate the average amount of money spent each month.

- What would be the value of $120,000 in a foreign country? Would you be able to buy more or less than you would here? Go online to research your answer. List your findings in a spreadsheet.

- How much would it cost to go to college in a foreign country? List the tuition and expenses in a spreadsheet.

Magazine Research

You've been given the task of compiling research for the school newspaper. Your assignment is to make a list of magazines in your school's library and create an informative table that will be helpful to the students of your school.

The editor has asked you to choose ten magazines from your library and summarize information about them. If your library has a limited selection, use the Internet to search for magazines.

Using database software, you will organize and list all your findings.

In this project you will:

- ☑ **Compile research using magazines from the library or using the Internet**
- ☑ **Create a table**
- ☑ **Sort the table alphabetically**

Project Curriculum Skills

Language Arts, Science, Social Studies

Compile the Research Data

1. Choose ten magazines from the library or the Internet that interest you.

2. For each magazine, write down the information you need to complete the table started in Figure 3-1.

Enter Data into Your Table

1. Use your database software to create a table with the field names listed in Figure 3-1.

2. Record the data about the ten magazines you chose.

3. Save the file.

4. Sort the table alphabetically according to *Name of Magazine*.

5. Now sort the list alphabetically by *Major Content Area*.

6. Save the file again.

SKILLS CHECK

If you need help with sorting, use your software's Help feature and your word processor to write the steps for sorting a table.

ID	Name of Magazine	Date of Issue	Major Content Area	Good Resource for Assignments In
1	Sports Illustrated for Kids	Winter, 2000	Sports	Wellness/fitness

Figure 3-1 Magazine data

Curriculum Connection

Choose a topic that you are currently studying in science class. Use the Internet or magazines to find at least five articles on this topic. Create a database to record the information you find. Which magazine has the most useful information? Is the information up to date? Write a short summary about something you learn from the articles.

Choose a current news topic. Find newspaper sites on the Internet or use the newspapers in your library. Read stories about this topic in the different newspapers. Are there differences in how the various newspapers report on this topic? Create a database using your research findings. Use the field names *Newspaper*, *Date*, *Topic*, and *Their View* as the fields in your database, or create your own field names.

Project

4

Striking It Rich!

It's **your lucky** day! Your school has received $25,000 from an unknown benefactor to use for technology purchases for your school. Your principal has asked the student council to provide a suggested shopping list. The money is for technology "extras" but not for computers, printers, and so on. It's time to go shopping!

In this project you will:

- ☑ **Use the Internet to compare prices**
- ☑ **Bookmark sites**
- ☑ **Create a spreadsheet with formulas**
- ☑ **Copy formulas**
- ☑ **Apply formats**
- ☑ **Merge cells**
- ☑ **Apply currency formatting**
- ☑ **Insert clip art**

Project Curriculum Skills

Language Arts, Mathematics

Research What to Buy

1. Use the Internet or newspapers to compare prices and shop for items.

2. If you are using the Internet for your research, bookmark the sites you visit for future reference.

3. Write down ten items you want to purchase and the price for each.

TIP

Use your Internet browser's Favorites or Bookmarks feature to save sites you visit often.

Create a Spreadsheet

1. Create a spreadsheet to record your purchases.

2. Enter a title for the spreadsheet.

3. Label the columns as shown in Figure 4-1.

4. Enter your data and save the spreadsheet.

5. Enter a formula in the Total column to calculate the cost of each item.

6. Copy the formula for the first item to the other nine items.

7. Enter a formula to calculate the Grand Total amount.

8. Format the Cost and Total columns as currency with two decimal places.

9. Use your software's merge feature to center the title across columns.

10. Increase the font size, add bold, and a fill color to the title.

11. Bold and center column headings and the Grand Total row heading.

SKILLS CHECK

If you're unsure how to copy the formula, use your software's Help feature and your word processor to write the steps to copy formulas.

SKILLS CHECK

If necessary, use your software's Help feature and your word processor to write the steps to merge cells.

Striking It Rich!

	A	B	C	D
1				
2	**Dearborn Middle School**			
3	**Technology Purchase Wish List**			
4				
5	**ITEM**	**QUANTITY**	**COST**	**TOTAL**
6	Large Screen TV	1	3200	= C6*B6
7	Digital Camera	3	499	= C7*B7
8	ITEM 3			
9	ITEM 4			
10	ITEM 5			
11	ITEM 6			
12	ITEM 7			
13	ITEM 8			
14	ITEM 9			
15	ITEM 10			
16				
17	GRAND TOTAL			Formula

Figure 4-1 Technology purchase spreadsheet

12. Apply a fill color to the column headings and the Grand Total row heading.

13. Insert clip art where appropriate.

14. Save the spreadsheet again.

Curriculum Connection

Language Arts

✔ Look in the weekend newspaper for store ads. Choose two stores that sell similar items. Read the ad and compare five or more products from each store. Look for special deals or offers in each advertisement. Create a spreadsheet to compare prices. Use graphics and format the spreadsheet to make it more attractive. Use your word processor to write a short paragraph explaining which stores you would buy from and why.

✔ Use presentation software to create a presentation for members of the school board to convince them to buy the items on your wish list. Your presentation should explain how each item would enhance learning. Include graphics in your presentation. Practice giving your presentation to your classmates and teacher.

Mathematics

Assuming you earn the minimum wage per hour, how many hours would you need to work to buy two items on your wish list? Assuming that you are in school from 7:30 a.m. to 3:00 p.m., Monday through Friday, how many days would it take you to reach the number of hours you need? Create a spreadsheet with two tables to answer each question.

Project 5

My Gradebook

Now that you are in middle school, you have more classes and more quizzes and tests than you did in elementary school. Keeping track of your grades is a great way to make sure you stay focused on your progress.

You will create a spreadsheet listing your last test, project, or quiz grade for each class. As the semester progresses, you will add more grades to the spreadsheet.

Using the information on your spreadsheet, you will create a chart and add elements to the chart.

In this project you will:

☑ **Create a spreadsheet**

☑ **Create a chart**

☑ **Format the chart**

☑ **Add a legend and data labels**

☑ **Insert clip art**

Project Curriculum Skills

Mathematics

Create the Spreadsheet

1. Make a list of your classes.

2. Next to each class, write your last test or project grade (use numbers).

3. Use your spreadsheet software, and enter the information as shown in Figure 5-1.

TIP

You may want to apply formats to the title and column headings. Apply a color fill where appropriate.

ANA'S GRADEBOOK, SEMESTER ONE	
CLASS/COURSE	TEST 1
English	89
Pre-Algebra	90
Science	95
Social Studies	80
Math	90

Figure 5-1 Gradebook spreadsheet

4. Format the spreadsheet and insert clip art to make it more attractive.

5. Save the spreadsheet.

Create the Chart

1. Highlight the data to be included in the chart.

2. Create a column or bar chart.

3. Change each bar to a different color.

4. Create a title for the chart with your name included.

TIP

If your software has a chart wizard feature, use the wizard to create the chart.

5. Insert data labels.

6. Insert a legend.

7. Save the spreadsheet again.

Time Spent on Task 20 minutes

Adding More Grades to the Spreadsheet

1. As the semester progresses, add test grades, quizzes, and any project grades.

2. Determine an average report card grade for each class. Use Figure 5-2 as an example.

ANA'S GRADEBOOK, SEMESTER ONE								
CLASS/COURSE	TEST 1	TEST 2	TEST 3	Average Test Grade	QUIZ 1	QUIZ 2	QUIZ 3	Average Quiz Grade
English	89	83	78	89	73	79	81	78
Pre-Algebra	90	87	78	90	85	86	90	87
Science	95	92	88	95	96	98	88	94
Social Studies	80	85	89	80	95	78	89	87
Math	90	89	93	90	90	80	85	85

Figure 5-2 Calculate an average grade

Curriculum Connection

In your assignment book, write down your test, quiz, and project grades as soon as they are returned. At the end of each week, list all the grades for each class, and calculate the average. Be sure to add all test grades together for one average and all quiz grades together for one average. Choose one class and determine what grade you need to receive on your next major test in order to end up with an A average.

Collect data from the Internet or other sources about the planets in our solar system. You might record data about temperature, distance from the earth, and size of the planets. Create a spreadsheet to record the data. Create a graph to illustrate differences between planets.

Choose three or more countries you are studying or have studied and collect data about the country from the Internet or from your library. Your research could include population, size of the country, and so on. Create a spreadsheet to record the data. Create a graph to illustrate your research.

Project 6

Net Wise

You want to become president of the Technology Club. One requirement for this position is that you must answer a few questions to determine your "Net knowledge."

The person with a perfect score will be the next president of the Technology Club.

Let's get started and see how much you know about the Net.

In this project you will:

☑ **Master the basics of the Internet**

☑ **Find information using effective search techniques**

☑ **Record data in a word processing file**

☑ **Apply format styles**

☑ **Insert clip art**

Project Curriculum Skills

Language Arts, Social Studies

Master the Basics

TIP

Multitask by keeping the Internet connection open as you answer the questions in your word processing file.

1. Open your Internet browser and go to *www.learnthenet.com*.

2. In the **HOW TO** section, click on **Master the Basics**.

3. Answer the following questions in a word processing file as you go through each section.

Monitor Settings

A. What is the best setting for your monitor? Why?

Netiquette

B. Why should you avoid using all caps in your e-mails?

C. What are emoticons? Give one example.

D. What is spamming?

E. What is flaming?

F. What are two abbreviations you can use in e-mail messages to shorten the text?

G. What are FAQs?

Birth of the Net

H. When and why did the Internet start?

Net Anatomy

I. What is the purpose of a chat room?

J. On the Internet, many different communications go on at the same time. Explain what this means.

The Future

K. What is bandwidth? Which technologies have increased bandwidth, or in other words, which technologies offer the fastest connections?

L. What is the Internet2?

M. How fast is the Internet2?

4. Save the document.

5. Add a title and format the document to make it attractive and interesting.

6. Add appropriate clip art.

7. Save the document again.

Time Spent on Task 60 minutes

The Interactive Search Engine Tutorial

1. Open your Internet browser and go to *www.learnthenet.com*.

2. In the **HOW TO** section, click **Find Information**.

3. Click the link **The Interactive Search Engine Tutorial**.

4. Go through this tutorial. Define, explain, or state an example of each term listed in Figure 6-2 in a word processing file.

5. Save the document.

6. Add a title and format the document to make it attractive and interesting.

7. Add appropriate clip art.

8. Save the document again.

NOTE

Read the terms shown in Figure 6-2 that you need to define before proceeding with the tutorial.

TIP

Keep the Internet connection open as you type the information into a word processing file.

URL	.com
.edu	Boolean operator
.org	truncation

Figure 6-2 Define terms

Glossary of Terms

1. Return to the home page of *www.learnthenet.com*.

2. Under **RESOURCES**, choose **Glossary**.

3. Define, explain, or state an example of each term in Figure 6-3 in a word processing file.

4. Save the document.

5. Add a title and format the document to make it attractive and interesting.

6. Add appropriate clip art.

7. Save the document again.

TIP

Remember to keep the Internet connection open as you work in your word processing file.

browser	hypertext
client	home page
computer virus	hotlist
cookie	http://
domain name	search engine
HTML	World Wide Web

Figure 6-3 Glossary terms

Curriculum Connection

Language Arts

Make a list of five authors. Use a search engine to find out facts about the early life of each author, before he or she began to publish. Use your word processor to record the facts. Choose one of the authors and write a 300-word report. Include footers, headers, and a title page for your report.

Create a database of books each author has written. Include the copyright years of each book, the publisher, and information about the author as fields in your database.

Mathematics

Using a metasearch engine, locate five sites that list math projects you can do. Make a list of these sites and bookmark them. Compare the sites you found with the sites your classmates found.

Science

Using a metasearch engine, locate five sites that list projects for the current topic you are studying in science. Make a list of these sites and bookmark them. Compare the sites you found with the sites your classmates found.

Social Studies

Using a metasearch engine, locate five sites that list projects for the current topic you are studying in social studies. Make a list of these sites and bookmark them. Compare the sites you found with the sites your classmates found.

Surf the Net

You've been asked to introduce the Internet to some middle school students who transferred to your school without much Internet experience. You've decided to begin by finding sites of interest to students your age. Then, you'll create a table to give them so that they can explore further on their own.

In this project you will:

- ☑ **Explore interesting Web sites**
- ☑ **Create a table**
- ☑ **Apply formats to a table**
- ☑ **Insert clip art**

Project Curriculum Skills

Social Studies

Discover Interesting Web Sites

TIP

You'll see and hear about Web sites during news broadcasts, advertisements, and other shows.

1. The next time you watch TV, have a pen and paper handy to find interesting sites for the students to explore. Write down four or more Web sites that are mentioned in programs and commercials.

2. Look through newspapers or magazines to find Web sites that you think will interest the students. Write down four or more Web sites.

3. Visit and explore each site on your list.

NOTE

Be sure to find a variety of sites that will interest a broad range of middle school students. Sites must be appropriate for school.

Create a Table

1. Use your word processing software to create a three-column table, as shown in Figure 7-1.

Web Site	Topic	Source
disney.go.com/disneypictures/atlantis/flash/index.html	Movie: *Atlantis, the Lost Empire*	TV commercial
launch.com	Discover new music	Teen magazine
thewb.com/charmed	TV show: "Charmed"	TV commercial
msnbc.com	News	NBC news

Figure 7-1 Web sites table

2. List each Web site you selected, its topic, and its source (name of TV show, magazine, etc.).

3. Apply attractive formats to your table. Center and bold column titles.

4. Add clip art.

5. Save the document.

Curriculum Connection

Language Arts

Take a few minutes to think about the procedure you used for visiting a Web site. What did you have to do to get there? Did you have to turn on the computer and start the Internet software? What is the next step? Use your word processing software, and create a numbered list of the steps you must take to get to a Web site. Be sure to make it clear and easy to follow for the inexperienced user. Format the document attractively and add clip art.

Social Studies

Watch the evening news. Make note of the TV station's URL. Visit that Web site, and explore the current events of the day. Use your word processor to create a Top 10 News List for today's news. Format the document attractively and add clip art.

Explore with NASA

You have a major research project for science class coming up soon. You need to choose a topic that interests you. You decide to explore the NASA Web site to get ideas for your topic.

In this project you will:

- ☑ **Explore the NASA Web site**
- ☑ **Record data in a word processing file**
- ☑ **Insert bullets**
- ☑ **Apply format styles**
- ☑ **Insert clip art**

Project Curriculum Skills

Science, Language Arts

Tropical Twisters

1. Go to the NASA Web site by entering this URL: *http://spacelink.msfc.nasa.gov*.

2. Choose **Cool Picks**.

3. In the search box at the bottom of the page, type *tropical twisters* and click **Search**.

4. Select the first item on the list, **Tropical Twisters**, dated November 29.

5. Explore the site. Be sure to view the virtual reality (VR) tours and video clips.

6. Using your word processing software and the information on this site, answer the following questions.

7. Use the bullet feature of your software. Type each question, followed by the answer.

   - How are hurricanes named?

   - What causes hurricanes to form?

   - What is a storm surge?

8. Save the document.

9. Insert appropriate clip art and add a title.

10. Format the title in bold and increase the font size.

11. Save the document again.

Timeline of the Universe

1. Use the Back button to return to the **Cool Picks** section. In the search box, type *timeline of the universe* and click **Search**.

2. Select **Origins: Timeline of the Universe**.

NOTE

Use the links at the bottom of each page to find the answers.

TIP

Click the magnifying glass in the bottom right corner of the pictures to view them in more detail.

NOTE

Be sure to explore this Web site frequently for fascinating information and fun activities.

3. Using your word processing software and the information on this site, answer the following questions.

4. Use the bullet feature of your software. Type each question, followed by the answer.

   - What is the Big Bang?

   - How are stars created?

   - What is a supernova?

   - What are the raw materials for DNA?

5. Save the document.

6. Insert appropriate clip art and add a title.

7. Format the title in bold and increase the font size.

8. Save the document again.

Curriculum Connection

Language Arts

Return to the NASA Web site home page, and choose **Hot Topics**. Here you will find current events related to science, technology, and education. Choose one article. Using your word processing program, write a paragraph that includes the article's title and describes the main ideas of the article in your own words. Add a title, apply attractive formats, and add clip art to the document.

Mathematics

Return to the NASA Web site home page, and choose **The Library** at the left. Next choose **Overview**, then choose **NASA Fact Sheets** toward the bottom of the page. Click each fact sheet and create a spreadsheet listing the fact sheets by category. Total the fact sheets in each category. Add a title, apply attractive formats, and add clip art to the document.

Social Studies

Return to the NASA Web site home page, and choose **The Library** at the left. Next choose **Overview**, then choose **NASA Fact Sheets** toward the bottom of the page. Here you will find a variety of interesting topics to explore. Choose **Technology Transfer Fact Sheets**, and explore five topics from the list. Using your word processing program, write a paragraph describing how NASA research has improved people's quality of life. Add a title, apply attractive formats, and add clip art to the document.

Dog and Pony Show

You decide to buy a dog, but not just any dog. The key is to find the perfect canine for you and your living situation.

After you find the perfect pooch, you'll need to think about a companion for it. Should it have two legs, four legs, wings, or all of the above?

Don't delay! It's time to do some online research.

In this project you will:

- ☑ **Use the Internet for research**
- ☑ **Record data in a word processing file**
- ☑ **Apply format styles**
- ☑ **Insert clip art**

Project Curriculum Skills

Language Arts

Internet Research for the Dog

1. Log on to the Internet and use several search engines to investigate three breeds of dogs that you think you'd like by answering the questions in step 2.

2. As you find information, type the question and your answer in a word processing file. Try some search engines that you don't use often.

   - What are the characteristics of the breed?

   - What type of temperament does the breed exhibit?

   - What is the general appearance (size, color, etc.) of the dog?

   - How can you contact the rescue organization for this breed?

3. Include the Web site URL you used for each search in your document.

4. Save the document.

5. Repeat the process and answer the questions for the second and third breeds.

6. After researching the three breeds, think about your lifestyle and characteristics and choose a breed that's right for you. Add the name of the breed you chose to your document.

7. Add a title and apply formats and graphics to your document to make it more attractive.

8. Save the document again.

NOTE

Bookmark sites that you like for easy reference.

NOTE

Be sure to visit the American Kennel Club Web site at *www.akc.org*.

Project 9

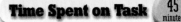

Internet Research for the Horse

1. Your dog is lonely when you go away, so you decide to get a horse for company. Once again you need to do some research.

2. Use several search engines to investigate two breeds that you think you'd like.

3. As you find information, type the question and your answer in a word processing file. Try some search engines that you don't use often.

   - What are the characteristics of the breed?

   - What type of temperament does the breed exhibit?

   - What is the general appearance (size, color, etc.) of the horse?

4. Save the document.

5. Repeat the process and answer the questions for the second breed.

6. Include the Web site URL you used for each search.

7. After researching the three breeds, think about your lifestyle and characteristics and choose a breed that's just right for you. Add the name of the breed you chose to your document.

8. Add a title and apply formats and graphics to your document to make it more attractive.

9. Save the document again.

Curriculum Connection

Make a list of books or magazines you have read recently that included animals. Use a search engine to find five uncommon facts about those animals. List the facts in a word processing document. Format the document attractively and add graphics.

Name an animal that is used for work in a foreign country. Use a search engine to find five facts about that animal. List the facts in a word processing document. Format the document attractively and add graphics.

Internet Scavenger Hunt

You have been given the important task of researching the answers to questions that are being used in a game show assembly at your school. The questions cover many subject areas and all the students in your class will be researching, too. Your goal is to get the most correct answers to the questions in the time allowed.

In this project you will:

☑ **Use and evaluate a variety of search engines**

☑ **Use the Internet for research**

Project Curriculum Skills

Language Arts, Social Studies, Math, Science

Internet Scavenger Hunt

The search engines listed in Figure 10-1 will help you when you have a topic to research, but they are not designed to find a specific address, or URL. When answering the questions for the scavenger hunt, try all these search engines. You will be asked to comment on them at the end of this project.

TIP

To go to the search engine, type the address on the Internet address line, and press Enter or Return. Then, type in the topic of your research and press the Search or Go button or press Enter or Return.

NOTE

There are many other search engines in addition to the ones on this list.

Search Engine Name	Address
AltaVista	www.altavista.com
Ask Jeeves	www.askjeeves.com
Dogpile	www.dogpile.com
Excite	www.excite.com
FinderSeeker	www.finderseeker.com
Google	www.google.com
HotBot	www.hotbot.com
Go.com	www.go.com
LookSmart	www.looksmart.com
Lycos	www.lycos.com
Mamma	www.mamma.com
Metacrawler	www.metacrawler.com
Starting Page	www.startingpage.com
WebCrawler	www.webcrawler.com
Yahoo	www.yahoo.com
GoTo	www.goto.com

Figure 10-1   Search engine sites

Use a variety of search engines from the list in Figure 10-1 to find the answers to the following questions. Fill in the chart neatly and completely. Be sure to use correct spelling.

Project 10

Question	Answer	URL (address) Where Found	Search Engine Used
1. Which U.S. president made Thanksgiving a national holiday?			
2. K-9 refers to a dog. K-6 refers to what?			
3. Who invented Velcro?			
4. HTTP stands for Hypertext Transfer Protocol; what does FTP stand for?			
5. How many baseball teams are in the American League?			
6. Your dog has Addison's disease. What is it and what treatment is available?			
7. Where in the U.S.S.R. was dancer Mikhail Baryshnikov born?			
8. Which breed of horse originated in Czechoslovakia? Clue: Only grays and blacks are bred today.			
9. How many gold medals did the U.S. women win in the Winter Olympics in Japan?			

Internet Scavenger Hunt

Question	Answer	URL (address) Where Found	Search Engine Used
10. Who invented the first steam engine and in what year?			
11. What does the literary device *foreshadowing* mean?			
12. Name 3 current events in the news today.			
13. What is a positive integer? What is a negative integer?			
14. What is the weather forecast for tomorrow for your area?			
15. What are the top 3 movies at the box office this week?			
16. What 4 countries share a border with the Czech Republic?			
17. What is the drug Reminyl® used to treat?			

10-2

Evaluate Search Engines

NOTE

You should evaluate all search engines on the list.

1. While working on the scavenger hunt, you used many different search engines. On the lines below, list and evaluate the search engines you used. Be sure to use correct spelling.

2. Answer the following questions for each search engine.

   • Did the search engine give you a variety of useful information?

   • Was the search engine easy to use?

   • Which search engine was your favorite? Why?

_____

_____

_____

_____

_____

_____

_____

_____

_____

_____

_____

_____

_____

_____

_____

_____

_____

Curriculum Connection

You need more language arts questions for the game show. Search online for famous quotations from literary classics. Choose two. Type two game show questions using the information you found. Your questions might sound something like this: "'To be or not to be: that is the question.' Name the literary classic where you'd find this quotation." Add a title, apply attractive formats, and add clip art to the document.

You discover that you need more questions relating to social studies for the game show. Include five questions about topics you are studying in social studies class to add to the scavenger hunt questions. Type the questions in your word processing software, and find the answers using your favorite search engine. Format the document attractively and add clip art.

You discover that you need more science questions for the game show. Ask your science teacher for a list of five questions from the curriculum to add to the scavenger hunt questions. Type the questions in your word processing software, and find the answers using your favorite search engine. Format the document attractively and add clip art.

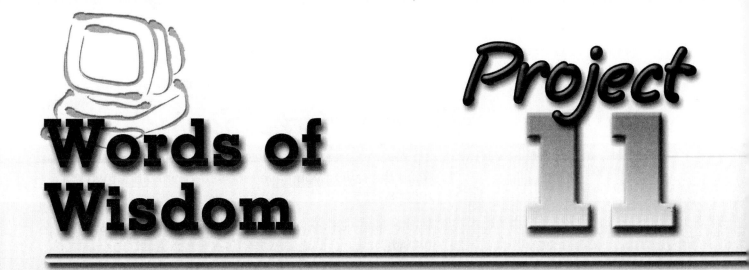

Words of Wisdom

Your teacher has decided to decorate the classroom with colorful posters that illustrate a variety of sayings. Each member of your class will pick a saying from a "grab bag" and create a poster to interpret and illustrate the saying.

In this project you will:

- ☑ **Interpret the message of a saying**
- ☑ **Design a poster to illustrate the message**
- ☑ **Set margins**
- ☑ **Use elements of design**

Project Curriculum Skills

Language Arts

Interpret the Saying

1. Read the saying you have received. Think about what it means.

2. In the space below, write your interpretation of its message.

_____

_____

Illustrate Your Saying

1. Now that you know what your saying means, you are ready to create a poster that illustrates the saying.

2. Use 8½ by 11-inch paper and set the margins to 0.75 inches.

3. Save the document.

4. Use clip art, word art, and colored text to create the poster.

5. Refer to the design elements chart shown in Figure 11-1. When creating a document, evaluate the design elements. Ask yourself these questions. Put check marks in the boxes as you evaluate your design choices.

6. Also consider using shapes and other elements on your drawing toolbar where appropriate.

7. Save the document again.

SKILLS CHECK

If you're unsure about how to set margins, use the Help screen of your software to learn how to set the margins.

	Is the purpose of the publication clear?
	Are graphics and fonts appropriate to the message?
	Is the publication organized?
	Is there a clear focal point?
	Was the audience considered when creating the publication?
	Is there consistency in the use of fonts, color, margins, and design elements?
	Is white space used appropriately?
	Is the publication original?

Figure 11-1 Design elements

Curriculum Connection

Language Arts

Talk to members of your family and your friends about sayings they have heard. Make a list of the sayings you have gathered. Interpret their meanings and share them with your class. Illustrate your document with appropriate graphics and apply attractive format styles.

Mathematics

"A penny saved is a penny earned." If you saved 200 pennies a month for the next 5 years, how much money would you accumulate? If you deposited your pennies in a savings account that earned 3% interest each year, how much would you have at the end of 5 years? Create a spreadsheet to make the required calculations. Format your spreadsheet attractively and add appropriate graphics.

Science

"An apple a day keeps the doctor away." Is there any scientific evidence to support this old saying? Do some online research to see if you can back up this saying with scientific fact. Does an apple contain elements that help to keep you healthy? Use your word processing program to write a paragraph summarizing your findings. Illustrate your paragraph with appropriate graphics and apply attractive format styles.

Part 2 Intermediate Projects

Project 12 — Buying the Ultimate Dream Machine

You have been saving your money for two years. Now you are ready to buy the ultimate computer system. When making a major purchase, always do your research and compare at least two items that are similar.

After completing your research, you will write an informative report explaining the features of each system and why those features are important to you. Then you will create a spreadsheet that compares the major features of each system and charts each feature. Using presentation software, you will present a summary of your findings to the class.

Project Curriculum Skills

Language Arts, Mathematics

In this project you will:

- ☑ Take notes on computer specifications
- ☑ Use the Internet or advertisements for research
- ☑ Write an informative report
- ☑ Create a spreadsheet
- ☑ Graph the data
- ☑ Prepare a presentation

Class Discussion and Note Taking

TIP

Use your word processing software to take notes.

1. Your teacher will lead a discussion about what to consider when buying a computer. Take notes on this information.

2. After the class discussion, think about how you will use your computer system now and in the future.

3. Choose between a laptop and a desktop system.

"Shop" for Your Computer System

TIP

Bookmark the sites you visit. You will need to cite the URLs later in this project.

1. Using the Internet or newspaper advertisements, choose two computers (either two laptops OR two desktops).

2. Choose a printer if one is not included. You may choose a multifunction printer. Other peripherals, such as scanners and joysticks, are optional.

3. Decide which of the two computers you will buy. If using newspaper ads, cut out your choices.

4. Use your word processing software to make a list of the software included.

5. Save the document.

6. Use the Internet to find out about customer service and support for your computer and for your printer.

7. Include three facts about the customer support in your document.

8. Save the document again.

Prepare an Informative Report

1. Using the information you gathered in activities 12-1 and 12-2, write a report using correct report format. Include the following information.

   - Brand and model of the two computers you compared.

   - The brand you chose to buy and the features it has.

   - Where you will buy it.

   - Why you chose the computer (refer to your notes from Section 12-1).

   - How you will use the computer.

   - What software is included.

   - Brand of printer included, or the brand and type you will buy.

   - Elaborate on the major specifications for your computer. Show that you know what the features mean.

   - Discuss the information you found on the Internet about service and support.

2. Create a title page for your report. Include your name, your teacher's name, the name of the class, and the date.

3. Insert an appropriate graphic on the title page.

4. Save the file.

NOTE

Be sure to cite your sources. List Internet sites also.

Create a Spreadsheet

1. Create a spreadsheet that compares the following information about the two computers you're researching.

CD, DVD, or CD-RW speed	Processor speed (MHz)	Monitor size	Total price
Modem speed	Hard drive size	RAM or DRAM	

2. List each feature of the system, including price. Refer to Figure 12-1 for a sample spreadsheet.

3. Save the file.

4. Format the spreadsheet attractively and add graphics.

5. Save the file again.

System	Dell	Gateway
CD-RW	10	12
Modem	56	56
Monitor size	17	19
Hard drive (gigabytes)	17	20
Processor speed (MHz)	800	933
RAM or DRAM	128	256
Price	1100	1250

Figure 12-1 Spreadsheet data

Time Spent on Task 30 minutes

Graph the Data

1. Create a chart comparing each feature listed above.

2. Use bar or column graphs. Refer to the sample graph in Figure 12-2.

3. Save the file again.

Buying the Ultimate Dream Machine

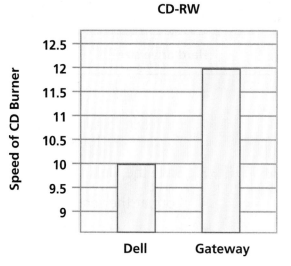

Figure 12-2 Comparison chart

Prepare a Presentation

1. Discuss the two computers and printer(s) you compared.

2. Prepare a presentation for the class.

3. Copy and paste the charts you created in Section 12-5 into your presentation. If necessary, resize the charts to fit the screen.

4. Explain which system you chose and why.

5. Save the file.

6. Present your slide show to the class.

Curriculum Connection

Read the business or technology sections of your local newspaper or use the Internet to conduct your research. Find two articles pertaining to technological innovations. Type your findings in a word processing file. Format the document attractively and include clip art.

Use the Internet or a newspaper to research careers in the technology field. List at least three careers with a description of each in a word processing file. What educational requirements are needed for each job? Format the document attractively and include graphics.

Research the cost of graphing calculators. Create a spreadsheet comparing features and prices. Format the spreadsheet and include graphics. Create a chart that compares the prices.

Project 13

The Money in My Pocket

You have been working part-time on weekends and in the summer. So far, it has been pretty simple. You get paid $5 for one hour; you go home with $5. When you get your first job, however, you must pay taxes on every dollar earned. How much money would you really be making if you were paying taxes?

You will create a spreadsheet that lists your hours worked and your pay. Using formulas, you will calculate taxes and your take-home pay. You will quickly see that the amount of money you make is not the same amount of money you take home!

In this project you will:
- ☑ **Create a spreadsheet**
- ☑ **Add formulas**
- ☑ **Use relative and absolute formulas**

Project Curriculum Skills

Mathematics

Create the Spreadsheet

1. Create a spreadsheet similar to Figure 13-1 to record your income.

2. Enter your own pay information into the spreadsheet. If you do not work, make up the data. If you receive an allowance, use those amounts.

3. Continue to enter data for a total of ten rows. You'll enter the Total Pay, Taxes, and Net/Take-Home Pay amounts in Section 13-2.

4. Save the file.

Johan's Part-Time Job				
Hours per Week	Rate of Pay	Total Pay	Taxes	Net/Take-Home Pay
5.0	$4.50			
6.0	$5.00			
3.5	$2.50			

Figure 13-1 Income spreadsheet

Enter the Formulas

1. Use a formula to calculate the Total Pay column in the spreadsheet you created in Section 13-1.

2. Use a formula to calculate the Taxes column.

3. Use a formula to calculate the Net/Take-Home Pay column.

4. Format the spreadsheet attractively. Be sure that all dollar amounts show two decimal places.

5. Save the file.

TIP

Use the formula wizard feature.

TIP

Use the edit/fill feature of your software to drag formulas down a column.

NOTE

Taxes are based on a percentage of your total pay. This percentage is referred to as the tax rate. You must multiply your tax percentage by the total pay to obtain the amount of taxes. The example shown in Figure 13-2 uses a 15% tax rate.

Johan's Part-Time Job				
Hours per Week	Rate of Pay	Total Pay	Taxes	Net/Take-Home Pay
5.0	$4.50	$22.50	$3.38	$19.13
6.0	$5.00	$30.00	$4.50	$25.50
3.5	$2.50	$8.75	$1.31	$7.44
4.0	$4.00	$16.00	$2.40	$13.60
7.0	$4.00	$28.00	$4.20	$23.80
6.0	$5.00	$30.00	$4.50	$25.50
5.5	$6.50	$35.75	$5.36	$30.39
4.0	$3.00	$12.00	$1.80	$10.20
7.0	$4.00	$28.00	$4.20	$23.80

Figure 13-2 Income after taxes

Computing Taxes Using Absolute Formulas

1. Copy the spreadsheet you created in Section 13-1 to cell A20.

2. Add the tax rate 0.15 (15%) above the Taxes heading.

3. Replace the existing tax formula with an absolute formula.

4. Change the tax rate to 0.20 (20%). Your amounts should change automatically.

SKILLS CHECK

If you're unsure about how to use absolute references, use your software's Help feature and your word processor to write the steps.

TIP

If the formula did not work, check to make sure the dollar signs used to create the absolute references are placed correctly.

Curriculum Connection

Create a spreadsheet similar to the one created in this project. Find the average rate of pay for all days worked. Then copy the table to cell A20 and find the average number of hours worked. Format the spreadsheet attractively and insert graphics.

Research the history of taxes in your state. Find the tax rates on income over the last decade. Enter these rates into a spreadsheet similar to the one created in this activity. Format the spreadsheet attractively and insert graphics. Create a chart with the data you gathered. Add a title and a legend to the chart.

Let's Go Shopping

Your **Key Club** has been assigned to work with the Red Cross to help victims of a hotel fire. You must stay overnight at the Red Cross center and provide your own meals. As club president, you have been given the task of grocery shopping for you and the club members. You can spend a maximum of $100. You will create a spreadsheet that lists the items, the cost of each, and the total. You will also determine the percentage of your total purchase for each item.

For club records, you will create a chart comparing the percentage of expenses to the total amount spent.

In this project you will:
- ☑ **Create a spreadsheet**
- ☑ **Use absolute references**
- ☑ **Create a chart**
- ☑ **Chart nonadjacent columns**

Project Curriculum Skills

Mathematics

Create the Spreadsheet

1. Use food ads or the Internet to find prices for groceries for the Key Club. Remember, you must buy enough food for the club, not just yourself.

2. Create a spreadsheet similar to Figure 14-1.

3. Enter your own information into the spreadsheet.

4. Use absolute references in the formula to determine percentages (see Figure 14-1).

5. Format the sheet attractively and add graphics. Be sure that all data is readable.

6. Save the file.

NOTE

Remember to keep your spending under $100.

TIP

Enter the sum formula first in the Total row and it will calculate as you enter each new grocery item.

SKILLS CHECK

If you're unsure about how to use absolute references, use your software's Help feature and your word processor to write the steps.

Stellar Middle School Key Club		
Item	Total	Percentage of Total Purchase
Lunchmeat	15.75	Formula
Snacks (chips, pretzels)	10.95	Formula
Ice cream	7.50	Formula
Frozen dinners	25.00	Formula
Total	Formula	Formula

Figure 14-1 Groceries spreadsheet

Create a Chart

1. Create an exploded pie chart that shows the item and the percentage of the total purchase it represents.

2. Be sure that your chart has a title and shows what each percentage represents. Each piece of the pie and each label must be readable.

3. Save the file.

NOTE

If available, use the chart wizard feature of your software.

Curriculum Connection

Mathematics

Talk with the treasurer of a school club. Ask him or her what the club's estimated expenses are for the year. Be sure to obtain the purpose of each expense and the dollar amount. Create a spreadsheet and chart similar to the one in this activity. Give the information to the club president.

Language Arts

Collect food ads from two or three local stores. Compare three similar items and their prices (for example, peanut butter, jelly, bread). Be sure to compare items by the same unit of measure. Create a spreadsheet listing each store, the items you compared, and the price. Highlight the store with the best prices. Create a chart and share your findings with the class.

Project 15 Finding Valid Web Sites

As the president of the Computer Club, you've been asked to help students in your school learn the difference between valid and invalid Web sites.

You have chosen the subject of animals and will explore a selection of sites to present to the students. You will need to find examples of both valid and invalid sites to show the students. You will use a form developed by your club advisor to determine the validity of the sites.

In this project you will:

- ☑ **Use the Internet for research**
- ☑ **Explore valid Web sites**
- ☑ **Identify invalid Web sites**

Project Curriculum Skills

Language Arts, Social Studies, Science

What Makes a Web Site Valid?

Review the *Finding a Valid Web Site* sheet shown in Figure 15-1. You will use these questions to determine if the sites you visit are valid or invalid.

Explore Web Sites

1. Visit the Web sites listed below. Then find at least two additional Web sites on any subject—one that is valid and one that is invalid.

    www.thefence.com/debate.asp?forumid=49 (Click **Read more** to view the whole article.)

    www.baldeagleinfo.com/

    www.allforanimals.com/index.htm

    www.manateeworld.net/ (Go to the site navigation menu.)

    www.seaworld.org

    www.nwf.org

2. Complete the form shown in Figure 15-1 for each site you visit. Be sure to use correct spelling and grammar.

TIP

It is easy to find invalid Web sites about controversial issues such as gun control, capital punishment, and the Holocaust.

Finding Valid Web Sites

Finding a Valid Web Site

Questions to Ask About a Web Page

1. Who is the author? Have you heard of the writer? Is he or she an acknowledged expert in the field? Have you heard of the organization that sponsors the site? Is it a reputable organization?

_____

_____

2. Is there a way to verify the legitimacy of the site (e.g., phone number, address to contact for more information)?

_____

_____

3. Is the article well written and grammatically correct?

_____

_____

4. Is there a non-Web version of this material?

_____

_____

5. What is the point of view? Most sites are not neutral. Consider the source of the information.

_____

_____

6. Are there references to other sources? Are they reputable sources?

_____

_____

7. Is there an indication of when the page was last updated? Newer information may be available.

_____

_____

Figure 15-1 Web site evaluation

Curriculum Connection

Using your word processing software, write a paragraph summarizing what you have learned about Web site validity. Were most sites you explored valid? Why or why not?

Science

Explore the issue of animal testing further. Be sure to use valid Web sites to collect your information. Do you believe that alternatives to animal testing should be required by law in place of tests using animals? Why or why not? Create a slide show presentation and present your views to your classmates. Try to persuade them to agree with your opinion.

Project 16

Stock Market Madness

You are working for Invincible Investments, Inc. Your company handles investments for the rich and famous. Your job is to comparison shop for one of your clients, Prince Brock E. Lee. Money is no object for the prince!

First, you must think of three areas to research. Select two companies to compare in each area.

Next, create a table using your word processing software. In the table, you enter each stock and its current prices per share.

Finally, you share the information with Prince Lee so that he can make a wise investment decision.

Project Curriculum Skills

Mathematics, Language Arts

In this project you will:

☑ **Use the Internet for research**

☑ **Summarize data in a table format**

Selecting Companies

1. A list of some of the popular industry areas and heavily traded stocks is shown in Figure 16-1. You may use this list or one provided by your teacher.

Fast Food	Restaurant Chains
McDonald's	Applebee's
Burger King	Outback Steakhouse
Wendy's	TGI Friday's
Internet	**Technology**
Yahoo	Intel
Lycos	Gateway
Amazon	Dell
Retail	**Pharmaceutical**
K-Mart	Merck
Wal-Mart	Pfizer
Sears	Johnson & Johnson

Figure 16-1 Company list

2. Choose three industry areas.

3. In each of the three areas, choose two companies.

4. Write your selections in a word processing file. You should have a total of six companies. You will need this information for Activity 16-2.

TIP

Some other industry areas are Home Appliances, Retail/Building, Communications, Clothing, and Entertainment.

Online Research

1. Go to yahoo.com. In the top half of the home page, you'll see links to different categories. Click **Finance/Quotes**.

2. After the page loads, click **Global Symbol Lookup**. In this box, type in the company name (you don't need to capitalize).

3. After you click **Search**, Yahoo returns with a list of possible ticker symbols.

4. Read the list and choose the one that applies to your company.

5. When you find it, click the symbol. A small chart appears.

6. Leave yahoo.com open and proceed to Activity 16-3.

Record Information in a Table

1. Create a table similar to the one shown in Figure 16-2.

2. Click **DayWatch** in the yahoo.com site.

NOTE

Keep the Internet site open as you are working on your table.

SKILLS CHECK

If you're unsure how to create a table, use your software's Help feature and your word processor to write the steps.

Company Name	Industry	Last Trade (price)	Day's Range (low to high)
Taco Bell	Fast Food		
McDonald's	Fast Food		
Intel	Technology		
Gateway	Technology		
Yahoo	Internet		
Amazon	Internet		

Figure 16-2 Stock prices table

3. In your table, record the **Last Trade** (price for which each share was recently sold).

4. Record the **Day's Range** (low and high prices).

5. Repeat this procedure for each stock.

6. Save the file.

7. Format the table and add graphics to your document.

8. Highlight in color the three stocks you would recommend to your client.

9. Save the file again.

Curriculum Connection

Language Arts

Go online and research the history of a company in your favorite industry (for example, clothing, music, sports, or ice cream). When was the company started? What is the purpose of the company, or what is its mission statement? Write a short summary of your findings in a word processing file.

Mathematics

Choose two stocks in the same industry. Create a table similar to the one in this activity. Record the final daily selling price for one week. At the end of the week, calculate the average selling price for each stock. Also, calculate the amount of increase or decrease in selling price per day.

Social Studies

Research the names of one international company that is listed on the New York Stock Exchange. Choose a company in a country you are studying or have studied. Use the Internet to research the financial history of the company in that foreign country. Write a short paragraph that explains your findings.

Science

Use the Internet to research one major environmentally responsible corporation trading on the New York Stock Exchange. One example of an environmentally responsible practice is UPS's use of recycled cardboard for its cartons. Write a one- to two-paragraph summary of your findings.

Create a Newsletter

You and a team of fellow students were selected to create a one-page newsletter for your school. You may include articles on a variety of topics or choose a theme for the newsletter and write articles on topics related to the theme. As part of this project, you will design the masthead for the newsletter and create an attractive layout.

In this project you will:

☑ **Work with a team of students to create a newsletter**

☑ **Write an article for a newsletter**

☑ **Design a masthead for a newsletter**

☑ **Select graphics and create a layout**

☑ **Edit a newsletter**

☑ **Meet deadlines set by your teacher**

Project Curriculum Skills

Language Arts

Team Meeting

Meet with your team to get organized. As a group, make the following decisions.

1. Select a person to be the recorder. This person will take notes at each meeting using your word processing software.

2. Decide on a theme for your newsletter. You may choose not to have a theme and to write about a variety of topics instead.

3. Assign article topics to each team member. Discuss the length of the articles. Your newsletter will be only one page long.

4. At the end of the meeting, review the notes to be sure they are correct, and print a copy of the notes for each team member.

Write Your Article

1. Begin the writing process by composing at the computer using your word processing software. Let your thoughts flow on the page, without concern for spelling, punctuation, or grammar. You will go back and work on mechanics later.

2. Save the file.

3. Spell check your work.

4. Read your work and begin to edit as you see errors or changes that need to be made.

5. Save the file again.

6. Print one copy of the first draft of your article.

Peer Editing

1. Meet with members of your team. Exchange your article draft with another person. Read and discuss each other's articles.

2. At your computer, edit your article again, bringing it closer to its final form.

3. Save the file.

4. Print one copy and give it to your teacher to review.

Design a Masthead

NOTE

A masthead is a design that includes the title of the newsletter at the top of the page. It may also include graphics.

NOTE

You may want to sketch a masthead design on paper before using your software to create it.

1. Meet with your team to begin the layout and design of the newsletter.

2. Look at mastheads from other newsletters or newspapers for ideas.

3. Choose a name for your newsletter.

4. Using your word processing or desktop publishing software, begin designing your masthead. Include the name of the newsletter and a graphic or design. Use special fonts and effects to make your masthead catch the eye of your readers.

5. Save the file.

Plan Your Newsletter

When your teacher has approved your articles and final editing is complete, you are ready to place the articles in the newsletter.

1. Using your software's special features, create columns in your newsletter, as shown in Figure 17-1.

2. Insert appropriate graphics to illustrate your articles.

3. As a team, finalize the layout of your newsletter.

4. Save the document.

5. When it is complete, print one copy.

6. Each member of the team should read the entire newsletter again to be sure it is complete and correct.

7. Print the final copy.

NOTE

The method of placing the articles will vary depending on the software you are using. Your teacher will give you instructions for this process.

SKILLS CHECK

If necessary, use your software's Help feature to learn how to create columns.

Figure 17-1 Sample newsletter

Curriculum Connection

Language Arts

Share your expertise with newsletters with a novice. Using your word processing software, make a list of tips for creating a newsletter. Think of helpful information for a person who is creating his or her first newsletter.

Mathematics

Calculate the time you spent on each part of your newsletter (sections 17-1 through 17-5). Create a spreadsheet that lists the time you and each of your team members spent on each part. Calculate total time spent on the newsletter by each team member. Format your spreadsheet attractively. Create a chart to illustrate time spent on task by each team member.

Social Studies

Go online to research a historical period of your choice. Choose a 10-year period, such as the 1810s or 1920s. Research the events of that time. Create a newsletter that reports on those events.

Science

Create a newsletter that reports important scientific events in the news. Use a newspaper or the Internet to find current information.

Project 18

Take a Vacation

Your parents have decided to take the family on a vacation next summer and would like your help in planning the trip. It's up to you to choose the destination and do the research. Then you'll present your findings to "sell" your parents on your choice.

In this project you will:

☑ **Use the Internet to research a travel destination**

☑ **Create a brochure**

☑ **Prepare a presentation on your travel destination**

Project Curriculum Skills

Language Arts, Social Studies, Science

Internet Research

1. Choose a country, city, or state that you would like to visit.

2. Use the Internet to research that location. Look for the information listed in Figure 18-1.

3. Save the data in a word processing file.

4. Use the following to get started.

   a. *www.travelocity.com* (Click **Go to Destination Guides**.)

   b. *www.lonelyplanet.com* (Click **Search**, and enter your destination.)

   c. Use a search engine to find information for your location.

   d. Bookmark the sites you visit.

Weather/climate	Currency (if different from ours)
Location	Population
Lodging	Sights
Entertainment	Airports

Figure 18-1 Research data

Create a Travel Brochure

1. Design a travel brochure for your vacation destination. Include the data listed in Figure 18-1, along with any other information you'd like.

2. Use landscape orientation and a three-column format.

3. Include graphics to illustrate your brochure.

4. Save the brochure.

Prepare a Presentation

1. Using the data you gathered in your research for Section 18-2, prepare a 10-minute slide show presentation for the class.

2. Include pictures you copied from Internet sites.

3. Include a title slide.

4. Use transitions and animation.

5. Be prepared to answer questions about your topic.

NOTE

Always be careful about using graphics copied from the Internet. Be sure to read the copyright information on a site before copying graphics.

SKILLS CHECK

If you're unsure how to use clip art from the Internet, use your browser's Help feature and your word processor to write the steps.

TIP

Practice giving your slide show ahead of time. Time yourself so that your presentation runs about 10 minutes.

Curriculum Connection

Language Arts

Choose a foreign country that you would like to visit. On the Internet, research its cuisine (food). Using your word processing software, write a paragraph describing the cuisine of the country you chose and the differences between their food and that of our country.

Mathematics

Choose five foreign countries that use a different currency than the United States. Use a search engine or travel Web sites to find out how to convert the foreign currency into U.S. dollars. Create a spreadsheet to convert the foreign currency to dollars.

Social Studies

Choose a foreign country that you would like to visit. On the Internet, research its culture. Using your word processing software, write a paper describing the culture of the country you chose and the differences between its culture and this one. Use the information from the other activities on this page to create a travel brochure about the country. Conduct more research if necessary. Your brochure should entice others to visit the country.

Science

Choose a foreign country. On the Internet, research its weather and climate. Write a short paragraph comparing the weather in the foreign country to that in the area where you live.

Project
19

Redesign a Label

Your aunt is an advertising account executive with Boneit Advertising. To encourage your creativity and to give you an idea of what designers do, she has asked you to redesign an existing label. It's a great opportunity to learn about target markets and elements of design. You will choose a label from an existing product and redesign it.

In this project you will:

☑ **Determine a target market for a product**

☑ **Explore the elements of design**

☑ **Design a product label**

Project Curriculum Skills

Language Arts, Social Studies

Internet, WP, DTP

Choose a Product

NOTE

When choosing a product, keep in mind that you will be designing a totally new label for the product. Only the information on the label will remain the same.

Choose a product that you have in your home. It could be a can of soup, a bar of soap, a CD cover, or any other item with a label no larger than 7 by 10 inches. You must be able to carry the item or its label to school.

Determine the Target Market

1. Using an Internet search engine, find the meaning of *target market*. Write the definition below.

   _____

   _____

2. Using the information you learned on the Internet, describe the people who use the product.

   a. What is their age range? _____

   b. What is their income range? _____

   c. What is their gender (male, female)? _____

   d. What is their level of education? _____

   e. What is their geographic location? _____

   _____

   f. What is their family size and lifestyle? _____

   _____

Redesign a Label

3. Now think about the features of your label that will attract the target market. Brainstorm ideas for your label design on the lines below. Consider colors, fonts, font size, and graphics. How can you design a label to attract the people in the target market?

_____

_____

Time Spent on Task 20 minutes

Elements of Design

Think about the following elements of design before you begin creating your label.

- Consider the audience or target market when creating your design.

- Be consistent in the use of fonts, color, margins, and other design elements.

- Make graphics appropriate to the message.

- Use white space appropriately.

- Create a clear focal point.

Time Spent on Task 90 minutes

Design a Label

1. Using your word processing or desktop publishing software, design an entirely new label for your product.

2. Keep your target market and the elements of design in mind as you design your label.

3. Refer to the design elements chart in Figure 19-1. When creating a document, evaluate the design elements. Put check marks in the boxes as you evaluate your design choices.

SKILLS CHECK

If you're unsure about how to create a custom-size page, use your software's Help feature and your word processor to write the steps.

4. Be sure to include all the information used on the original label.

5. Make the label the same size as the original label.

6. Include color and graphic elements in your design.

7. Make changes if necessary.

8. Save the file.

	Is the purpose of the label clear?
	Are graphics and fonts appropriate to the message?
	Is the label organized?
	Is there a clear focal point?
	Was the audience considered when creating the label?
	Is there consistency in the use of fonts, color, margins, and other design elements?
	Is white space used appropriately?
	Is the label original?

Figure 19-1 Design elements

Curriculum Connection

Look at the labels on at least five different products. Using your word processing software, describe the label elements you find appealing and unappealing. Survey five other people and list their likes and dislikes. Create a spreadsheet to record the data. Graph the results.

You were chosen to redesign a label for a tube of toothpaste. The toothpaste will be marketed to both young people and senior citizens. Use your word processing or desktop publishing software to design two labels, one for each target market. In a separate document, describe in detail the differences between the labels. Explain why you chose the elements for each.

Examine a label on a package of food in your home. Using the Internet and your word processing software, answer the following questions about food labeling.

✔ What information is included about the package contents?

✔ Why is it important to the consumer to know the nutritional facts about the product?

✔ What organization regulates food labeling?

✔ What information is required by law?

Advertising Campaign

You did such a great job for your aunt in the last project, she has asked for more examples of your work. This time, you will prepare a complete advertising campaign for a product or service of your choice. You'll team up with a partner to help get the job done.

In this project you will:

☑ Create an advertising campaign

☑ Determine a target market

☑ Create a magazine ad

☑ Create a poster

☑ Create a billboard

☑ Create a coupon

☑ Create a radio script

☑ Create a presentation

Project Curriculum Skills

Language Arts, Social Studies

Choose a Product

You and your partner must first choose a product or service for your advertising campaign. Products could include a CD, a computer game or software, a skateboard, or a clothing item. Services could include a babysitting service, a lawn service, or a cleaning service. Choose a product or service that both members of the team can relate to.

NOTE

When choosing your product or service, be sure it is appropriate for school.

Determine the Target Market

Using the information you learned about target markets in Project 19, think about the people who use your product or service.

- What is their age range?

- What is their income range?

- What is their gender (male, female)?

- What is their level of education?

- What is their geographic location?

- What is their family size and lifestyle?

Team Meeting—Project Assignments

1. Each member of your team will create two of the advertising pieces. Decide who will create each of the advertising pieces, and record below.

   Magazine ad _____

   Billboard _____

   Poster _____

   Manufacturer's coupon _____

TIP

You can use the copy and paste features to copy logos and graphics from one file to another.

2. Now your team must develop some common themes and elements to carry throughout your campaign. Graphics, logos, and colors should be consistent in all the advertising pieces. Keep in mind the target audience while creating your designs.

3. Use a word processor to create your ad. Remember the important elements of design listed in Figure 20-1 as you develop your ad. Put check marks in the boxes as you review your ad.

4. Save the ad.

5. Insert a page break in your document to start a new page.

	Is the purpose of the publication clear?
	Are graphics and fonts appropriate to the message?
	Is the publication organized?
	Is there a clear focal point?
	Was the audience considered when creating the publication?
	Is there consistency in the use of fonts, color, margins, and other design elements?
	Is white space used appropriately?
	Is the publication original?

Figure 20-1 Design elements

6. On the new page, write a paragraph for each ad that includes details about that piece. In your paragraphs, answer the following questions.

- Where will your billboard be located? Why?

- In what magazines will you run your ad? Why?

- Where will your posters be displayed? Why?

- In what publications will you place your coupon? Why?

7. Save the ad again.

Radio Script

1. Working with your teammate, use your word processor to write a script to be read on the radio to advertise your product or service.

a. Keep your target market in mind as you write.

b. Describe the number of listeners, their age groups, and their genders.

c. "Set up" the ad by describing the tone (drama, comedy, etc.).

d. Describe the type of radio station that will run your ad (easy listening, rock, etc.).

2. Save the script.

Presentation

1. Using your presentation software and working with your partner, prepare a 10-minute presentation for your advertising campaign.

a. Create a title slide.

NOTE

Practice your presentation ahead of time. Time yourself so that your presentation runs about 10 minutes.

b. Create a slide describing your product or service and its target market.

c. Copy and paste all four ads into the presentation.

d. Copy and paste the information you wrote about each advertising piece into the presentation.

e. Prepare to perform your radio ad by reading the script with your partner.

2. Save the presentation.

3. Apply formats and graphics to your presentation to make it more attractive.

4. Use Figure 20-1 to evaluate your design choices. Put another set of check marks in the boxes as you review your presentation.

5. Make changes if necessary.

6. Save the presentation again.

Curriculum Connection

Using your word processing software, discuss what you have learned about target markets. Why is it important to know the target market before creating an advertising piece?

Interview at least ten people of various ages. Prepare several questions in advance about their willingness to purchase your product or service and the appeal of your ads. Describe your product or service, and present your four advertising pieces. Create a spreadsheet and graph that illustrate their responses by age group. Format the spreadsheet attractively and add graphics.

Advertising for a product varies greatly in different countries. Assume you will be creating an advertising campaign for a new soda that will be marketed in Japan and in Latin America. Use the Internet to research the differences in these cultures. Using your word processing software, write a paper describing the differences in your advertising campaigns for the two markets.

Part 3 Advanced Projects

Project 21
Find a Summer Job

You **want to** earn some spending money, so you have decided to get a summer job. You begin by researching the places you'd like to work. Then, you write a letter of application and create a resume. Finally, you use mail merge to print letters to prospective employers.

In this project you will:

☑ Write a personal business letter to apply for a summer job

☑ Use the mail merge feature of your software

☑ Create a resume

Project Curriculum Skills

Language Arts

Letter of Application

NOTE

A letter of application should contain three parts.
- ✔ Part 1—Explain how you learned about the position; be specific about the position you are pursuing.
- ✔ Part 2—Explain how you are qualified for the position and how you can be an asset to the company.
- ✔ Part 3—Request an interview.

1. Choose five businesses you'd like to apply to for a summer job.

2. Use a phone book to find their mailing addresses.

3. Use your word processor to write a letter to apply for a position. Use a letter template to create the letter.

4. Use the example in Figure 21-1 for formatting and for ideas for letter content.

5. Save the letter.

Sandra Rodriguez
27598 Lawrence Street
Pleasantville, PA 18789
March 21, 20—

Ms. Jean Sanders
Personnel Director
Sanders Gift Shops, Inc.
219 Cuyahoga Avenue
Pleasantville, PA 18789

Dear Ms. Sanders:

Mr. Andrew Bricson, Director of Marketing for Sanders Gift Shops, informed me of a summer cashier position in your Pleasantville shop. I believe I have the necessary qualifications and would like to be considered for this position.

I am a student at Jamison Middle School, where I work as a cashier in the school store. This job requires that I deal with the public, operate a cash register, and maintain an inventory. In addition, I have excelled in my keyboarding, computer applications, and word processing courses. In the future, I would like to work in the retail field. I am enclosing a resume with further details about my qualifications.

I would appreciate the opportunity to speak with you regarding this position. Please contact me at (523) 555-2332 to arrange an interview.

Sincerely,

Sandra Rodriguez
Enclosure

Figure 21-1   Letter of application

Mail Merge

1. Use the mail merge feature of your software to merge your letter to the five addresses you obtained from the phone book.

2. Save the file.

SKILLS CHECK

If necessary, use your software's Help feature and write the steps for creating a mail merge.

Resume

1. Create a resume in your word processing program. Use the sample resume in Figure 21-2 as a guide.

2. Save the resume.

TIP

Formatting Suggestions for Resumes
- ✔ Use an easy-to-read font style and size. Font size should not be smaller than 12 points on most documents.
- ✔ Make your headings and titles stand out by changing the font size, style, shape, or color.
- ✔ Center titles when appropriate.

SANDRA RODRIGUEZ
27598 Lawrence Street
Pleasantville, PA 18789
(523) 555-2332

EDUCATION
Jamison Middle School   7th Grade Honors Student
Business and Technology Courses   Keyboarding
                                    Computer Applications
                                    Word Processing

SCHOOL ACTIVITIES
Honor Roll, grades 6, 7
Member of the Computer Club, grades 6, 7
7th Grade Class President
Field Hockey Captain

WORK EXPERIENCE
Cashier, Jamison Middle School Store. Work 5 mornings per week before school. Operate cash register, assist customers, maintain inventory.

Babysitter, Mr. and Mrs. John Morales. Work weekends and evenings caring for two children, ages 4 and 6.

REFERENCES
Mrs. Rita Jones, School Store Advisor, Jamison Middle School, 56 Erie Street, Oakville, PA 18977.

Mr. and Mrs. John Morales, 18 Easton Avenue, Oakville, PA 18977.

Mr. Earl Bergman, Hockey Coach, Jamison Middle School, 24 West Street, Oakville, PA 18977.

Figure 21-2   Sample resume

Curriculum Connection

Language Arts

Use a personal letter format and the mail merge feature of your software to write a letter to five friends or family members.

Science

You are considering a future career in science. Do some online research to find at least five jobs or careers relating to science. Use your word processing software to create a table listing at least five careers in science, with their educational requirements.

Mathematics

Think about careers that interest you. Choose five careers to research online. Create a spreadsheet that contains the following headings: Career, Minimum Income, Maximum Income, Years of Education. Calculate the total minimum and maximum income for each career for a 10-year period.

Social Studies

Conduct online research about interviewing dos and don'ts. How should you dress? How can you prepare for an interview? Use your word processing software to create a table listing at least six job interview tips.

Voice Your Opinion

Project 22

As a member of the debate team, you will write a persuasive paper on one of a list of topics or, with your teacher's approval, on a topic of your choice. Your paper must convince the class and your teacher of your position.

You also will create a bumper sticker to express your views and then survey others about your topic. Use a spreadsheet to record the survey and graph the results. You will use presentation software to present your project to the class so as to inform and "sell" others on your view.

In this project you will:
- ☑ Use the Internet for research
- ☑ Write a persuasive paper
- ☑ Create a bumper sticker
- ☑ Conduct a survey
- ☑ Create a spreadsheet
- ☑ Graph the data
- ☑ Prepare a presentation

Project Curriculum Skills

Language Arts, Social Studies

Internet Research and Persuasive Paper

1. Choose a topic from the list below or pick a topic of your own and have it approved by your teacher.

Violence in schools	Smoking in public areas
Environment	Immigration
Capital punishment	Cloning
Energy	The right to bear arms
Health care	Protection of endangered species
Race relations	Animal testing
Military spending	Religion in the schools
Abortion	Educational reform
Violence in music lyrics	Taxes
Violence in movies and television	Censorship
Job equity	

2. Use the Internet to research the topic you chose.

3. Find at least three valid sources on the Internet. Use the worksheet shown in Figure 22-1 to determine if a site is valid.

NOTE

If the Web site is valid, you should be able to answer most of the questions in Figure 22-1. If you can't find answers to most of the questions, the site is probably not valid.

Finding a Valid Web Site

Questions to Ask About a Web Page

Authority

1. What company, organization, or individual is sponsoring the page?

_____

_____

2. Is there a way to verify their legitimacy (e.g., phone number, address to contact for more information)?

_____

_____

3. Is there a non-Web version of this material?

_____

Accuracy

1. Are sources for factual information clearly listed so they can be verified by another source? Name at least two sources.

_____

_____

2. Is the information free of grammatical, spelling, and typographical errors?

_____

Objectivity

1. Is the informational content clearly separated from the advertising and opinion content?

_____

2. Are the editorials and opinion pieces clearly labeled?

_____

Currency

When was the page last updated?

_____

Figure 22-1   Web site validity worksheet

4. Write a 200-word persuasive paper to convince the class and your teacher of your beliefs.

5. Be sure to footnote quotations and statistics and include a bibliography page in the correct format. See Figure 22-2 for a sample bibliography format.

6. Save the file.

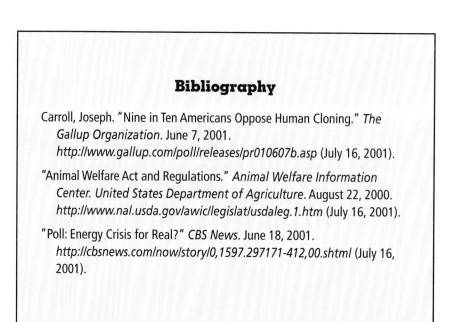

Bibliography

Carroll, Joseph. "Nine in Ten Americans Oppose Human Cloning." *The Gallup Organization.* June 7, 2001. *http://www.gallup.com/poll/releases/pr010607b.asp* (July 16, 2001).

"Animal Welfare Act and Regulations." *Animal Welfare Information Center. United States Department of Agriculture.* August 22, 2000. *http://www.nal.usda.gov/awic/legislat/usdaleg.1.htm* (July 16, 2001).

"Poll: Energy Crisis for Real?" *CBS News.* June 18, 2001. *http://cbsnews.com/now/story/0,1597.297171-412,00.shtml* (July 16, 2001).

Figure 22-2   Sample bibliography

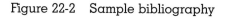

Time Spent on Task 45 minutes

Create a Bumper Sticker

1. Use your desktop publishing or word processing software to create a bumper sticker that expresses your views.

2. Refer to the design element chart in Figure 22-3. Put check marks in the boxes as you evaluate your design choices.

3. The bumper sticker should measure 4 by 10 inches with margins of 0.65 inch.

4. Remember that it must clearly communicate your message from a distance.

5. Save the file.

	Is the purpose of the publication clear?
	Are graphics and fonts appropriate to the message?
	Is the publication organized?
	Is there a clear focal point?
	Was the audience considered when creating the publication?
	Is there consistency in the use of fonts, color, margins, and design elements?
	Is white space used appropriately?
	Is the publication original?

Figure 22-3   Design elements

Time Spent on Task 120 minutes

Graph the Survey Results

1. Using your word processing software, write a survey with questions about your topic that can be answered yes or no. Have your teacher approve the questions and survey form before you make copies.

2. Include a section for interviewees to check their age group, but don't ask their exact age.

3. Survey at least twenty people of varying ages.

4. Design a spreadsheet to record the responses. A sample spreadsheet is shown in Figure 22-4.

5. Use the graph feature of your spreadsheet software to graph each question using a chart that clearly illustrates the results of the survey.

6. Include the questions on the graph.

7. Save the spreadsheet.

NOTE

Be sure to survey people from each age group.

TIP

Planning a spreadsheet is important. Try sketching your spreadsheet on a piece of paper before working at the computer.

If you are not sure how to create a chart, use your software's Help feature and write the steps for creating a chart.

	A	Ages 11-13	Ages 14-16	Ages 16-20	Ages 20-25	Ages 25-30	Ages 31-40	Ages 41-55	Ages 56+
3	Question 1								
4	Question 2								
5	Question 3								
6	Question 4								
7	Question 5								
8	Question 6								
9	Question 7								
10	Question 8								
11	Question 9								
12	Question 10								

Figure 22-4 Sample survey result table

Conclusions

Do you see any age-related or gender-related influences in their responses? Explain the differences.

_____

_____

_____

Time Spent on Task 45 minutes

Presentation

1. Prepare a 10-minute presentation for the class.

2. Include your survey questions and graphs illustrating the results.

3. Present the conclusions you drew from the survey, your research, and your bumper sticker.

4. Use the presentation not only to inform but also to "sell" your classmates and your teacher on your side of the issue.

5. Be prepared to answer questions about your topic and to lead or moderate a discussion among class members.

TIP

Practice your presentation ahead of time. Time yourself so that your presentation runs about 10 minutes.

Curriculum Connection

During your Internet research, you have discovered many Web sites focused on your topic. Which Web site did you prefer as a source? Why? Using your word processing software, write a paragraph describing your favorite site. Consider validity, wealth of information, ease of use, and visual appeal.

List the Web sites you visited for your research in a spreadsheet. Rate each site as valid or invalid based on the information in Figure 22-1. Total the number of valid and invalid sites.

Science

Many of the controversial topics on the list in Section 22-1 have a connection to science. Using your word processing software, create a table listing these topics, and add any other science-related topics you can think of. Which of those topics do you feel is the most pressing issue? Why? Arrange and number the topics in your table in order of importance to you. Below the table, write a paragraph explaining the reasons for your ranking.

Not all cultures view controversial issues in the same way. For example, in India, certain animals are sacred and would never be used for testing purposes. In some other cultures, animals are not valued, and their use in testing would be acceptable. Using your word processing software, make a list of five of the topics in Section 22-1. Next to each topic, describe cultural views of these topics that may differ from the views of Americans.

Project 23

Let's Eat!

You and your partner are entering the restaurant business! With your partner, you will plan and design the restaurant down to the smallest detail. You will design its letterhead, business cards, and Web page. You will also prepare a mailing to prospective financial backers.

In this project you will:

☑ **Create a detailed plan for a new restaurant**

☑ **Create a letterhead and business card**

☑ **Use the mail merge feature of your software**

☑ **Create a menu**

☑ **Design a Web page**

Project Curriculum Skills

Language Arts, Social Studies

WP, DTP, WPD

Brainstorm

NOTE

While making notes, be sure to give as much detail as possible.

Work with your partner to brainstorm the following items. As you brainstorm, use your word processor to make notes at your computer. You will use your notes in the next section.

1. What is the location of your restaurant—urban, suburban, or rural?

2. What type of restaurant is it—diner, drive-in, gourmet, trendy, deli, cafe, theme restaurant, or other?

3. What type of clientele will you draw? Who is your target market?

4. Describe the exterior in detail. When patrons approach your restaurant, what will they see?

5. Describe the atmosphere and décor inside the restaurant. Use shape and drawing tools to draw the layout. What colors will you use?

6. Details, details, details! What else can you tell us about your restaurant?

Save the notes file.

Formal Restaurant Description

Work from your brainstorming notes to type up a formal, detailed description of the restaurant based on the six questions in Section 23-1. The description should be presentable for prospective investors. Save your description file.

Letterhead and Business Card

TIP

A business card measures 3.5 by 2 inches. The top section of your letterhead should be no more than 1.5 inches deep. The bottom section of your letterhead should be no more than 0.75 inch deep.

1. Using color, special fonts, graphics, and your software's drawing tools, design a letterhead and business card for your restaurant. Be sure to use the same design elements in both, so that there is a common theme.

2. Save your design.

3. When your design is complete and you have proofread it carefully, print five copies.

Letter and Mail Merge

NOTE

Be sure to use correct business letter format.

1. Write a letter to be mailed to prospective investors in your restaurant.

2. Make sure your letter includes the following.

   a. Brief description of the restaurant

   b. A summary of the abilities of your partner and yourself

   c. Request for financial backing

   d. Request for a meeting to discuss your plans

3. Save the letter.

4. Enclose the formal, detailed description you created in Section 23-2 with the letter.

5. Choose five names and addresses from the phone book or another source. Use your word processing software's mail merge function to merge your letter to the five addresses. Be sure to proofread carefully before printing the letters on the letterhead you created in Section 23-3.

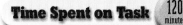

Menu

1. Begin with a sketch of your menu. Will the menu be on a whole sheet of paper or in a book format, folded down the middle? Sketch your ideas on the paper.

2. Use your ideas from the sketch to create a menu in your word processing or desktop publishing software. Use the elements of design as a guide. Remember that the menu must fit the restaurant and the clientele you plan to attract and should encourage people to eat at your restaurant.

3. Save your design.

4. Refer to the design element chart in Figure 23-1. Ask yourself these questions when you create the menu. Put check marks in the boxes as you evaluate your design choices.

SKILLS CHECK

If necessary, use the software's Help menu to learn how to create a book format for your menu.

NOTE

You may want to research prices in restaurants similar to yours as you create the menu.

	Is the purpose of the publication clear?
	Are graphics and fonts appropriate to the message?
	Is the publication organized?
	Is there a clear focal point?
	Was the audience considered when creating the publication?
	Is there consistency in the use of fonts, color, margins, and design elements?
	Is white space used appropriately?
	Is the publication original?

Figure 23-1   Design element chart

Let's Eat!

Web Page

NOTE

Remember: Always keep your target market in mind.

1. Design a Web page for your restaurant. Remember to carry your common theme throughout the Web page.

2. Your Web page should include the following.

   a. A description of your restaurant

   b. The location

   c. The menu

   d. Any other elements you'd like

3. Use the elements of design listed in Figure 23-1 in developing the Web page.

4. Save your Web page.

Curriculum Connection

Social Studies

As a restaurant owner, you will have many employees. Go online to research laws related to hiring practices. Use your spreadsheet software to create a list of at least three relevant regulations and the dates they became law.

Language Arts

Using your word processing software, write a radio advertisement to publicize the grand opening of your restaurant.

Science

Now that you are in the food business, you must be concerned with public safety. Go online to determine what regulations you must follow for the safe handling of food. List at least three regulations. What organization will inspect your restaurant to be sure you are within the law?

Project 24

Trendy Travel Agency

You own and operate Trendy Travel Agency. Intelligent Corporation will host a one-week sales convention in Europe, Asia, or Australia. Penelope Smart, CEO of Intelligent Corporation, has asked you to prepare a travel plan for her sales force.

You will use the Internet for your research and create a comparison chart using spreadsheet software. You will prepare a table that lists each city, its currency name, and the exchange rate. You will create a database of the ten employees at this conference. Finally, you must share all your findings with Ms. Smart using presentation software.

Project Curriculum Skills

Language Arts, Mathematics, Social Studies, Science

In this project you will:
- ☑ **Research cities**
- ☑ **Write summaries**
- ☑ **Create a spreadsheet**
- ☑ **Research airfares**
- ☑ **Create a graph**
- ☑ **Research foreign currency and exchange rates**
- ☑ **Create a table**
- ☑ **Make a database of addresses**
- ☑ **Create a presentation**

Research Cities

Time Spent on Task 60 minutes

1. Use the Internet to research three cities you are studying in social studies or three cities of your choice. Each city must be on a different continent.

2. Use different search engines to find the cities and bookmark the sites as you are surfing.

3. Keep the Internet connection open for Section 24-2.

Write Summaries

Time Spent on Task 60 minutes

NOTE

Keep each item of information to one paragraph.

TIP

Look for a link on the weather page for that city that points to records and averages or something similar.

1. Using word processing software, summarize the first city you chose, and include the following information.

   a. History and culture

   b. Points of interest

   c. Weather patterns throughout the year

2. Check your spelling and grammar.

3. Save the file.

4. Create a new file for each city.

5. Repeat steps 1 through 3 for each city.

6. Save the files.

Create a Spreadsheet

Time Spent on Task 15 minutes

1. Create a spreadsheet as shown in Figure 24-1.

2. Save the file.

	A	B	C
1	City	Roundtrip Airfare per Person	Airlines
2			
3			
4			

Figure 24-1   City comparison chart

3. Leave the file open, but minimize it.

4. You will record pricing information in this spreadsheet in Section 24-4.

Time Spent on Task 45 minutes

Research Airfares

1. Use *www.travelocity.com* to find roundtrip airfares for each of your three cities.

   a. Use a major city near you for departure information.

   b. Length of stay is seven days.

   c. Use any dates.

2. Go back to the travel sites you bookmarked in Section 24-1.

3. Record your findings in the chart you created in Section 24-3.

Time Spent on Task 20 minutes

Create a Graph

1. Create a bar or column graph to compare the airfares from Section 24-4.

2. Save the chart.

TIP

Use the chart wizard feature of your software.

Research Foreign Currency and Exchange Rate

1. Go to *www.exchangerate.com*.

2. Bookmark this site.

3. On a piece of paper, write down the three cities you researched, the currency used, and the exchange rate.

Create a Table

1. Use your word processor to create a table that lists the currency information (refer to Figure 24-2).

2. Type the data collected in Section 24-6 into this table.

3. Save the file.

City	Currency	Exchange Rate to the U.S. Dollar

Figure 24-2   Currency exchange rate table

Create a Database

1. Use database software to create a list of employees attending the conference. Use the field names shown in Figure 24-3.

Last Name	First Name	Street	City	State	Country	ZIP	Phone Number

Figure 24-3   Field names

SKILLS CHECK

If necessary, use your software's Help feature to review how to create a database.

2. Add data for ten employees. Make up the names, addresses, and other information.

3. Sort alphabetically by last name.

4. Resize the columns so that all words and letters are visible.

5. Save the file.

TIP

Use the Sort button on your toolbar if available.

24-9

Time Spent on Task 60 minutes

Create a Presentation

1. Create a slide show with five or six slides that summarizes your findings. Be prepared to explain the chart and table.

2. Include the following.

    a. Part of each city's summary from Section 24-2. Include only some points of interest, city history, and weather.

    b. Graph from Section 24-5.

    c. Table from Section 24-7.

    d. Your recommendation and why you chose that city.

3. Save the presentation.

4. Practice your presentation.

5. Give your presentation to the class.

Curriculum Connection

Research a city mentioned in a recent novel. How could you persuade someone to visit this city? In a word processing file, write an outline for a persuasive paper.

Use the Internet to research the food or dress of three foreign cultures. Design a table to record your information.

Think of three items you would like to buy and the cost of each. Using the exchange rates you researched in this project, calculate how much it would cost to purchase each item with each currency.

Research the weather patterns where you live. Compare them to the weather patterns of the foreign cities you researched.

Project 25
Dilemmas and Decisions with Data

Because of your expertise in using database software, your teachers have asked you to create a database of topics for English, social studies, math, and science classes.

You will brainstorm possible topics and then choose the topic and the purpose of the table. Using database software, you will create the database and enter the data. You will create one table for each of the four subjects. You will then create two queries for each table. Finally, you will make a brief oral presentation to the class explaining what you did for this project.

In this project you will:

- ☑ **Design a table**
- ☑ **Compile data**
- ☑ **Record data**
- ☑ **Create queries**
- ☑ **Make an oral presentation**

Project Curriculum Skills

Language Arts, Mathematics, Social Studies, Science

Decide on a Topic and Data

1. Choose a topic for each of these subject areas: English, social studies, math, and science.

2. Choose data to list for that topic.

3. Make a list of your topics and data.

Design Your Tables

1. Use your database software to design a table for each subject.

2. Choose appropriate field names, as shown in Figure 25-1.

3. Enter the data for each of the four tables.

4. Save the file.

TIP

To save time, create one file but a new table for each subject.

TIP

If you make a mistake, you will be able to add, delete, or edit any field name after the table is created.

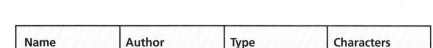

Name	Author	Type	Characters

Figure 25-1   English topic: books on reading list

Create Two Queries for Each Table

1. Brainstorm possible queries for each table. A query for a book list might be to select all the fiction you have read in a certain period of time and the author of each book.

Dilemmas and Decisions with Data

SKILLS CHECK

If necessary, use your soft-ware's Help feature and list the steps to create a query.

2. Decide on two queries for each table.

3. Run the queries for each table.

4. Save each query.

Time Spent on Task 60 minutes

25-4 Make an Oral Presentation to the Class

1. Use the outline feature of your word processing software to outline all the steps in this project.

2. Save the file.

3. Give a five-minute oral report to the class explaining what you did to complete this project.

TIP

Be sure to mention each table and the queries you created.

NOTE

Practice before you present!

Curriculum Connection

List ten of your favorite authors. Research each author's life and find an interesting fact about him or her. Choose something you don't already know about the author. Create a table that lists first name, last name, and personal fact. Enter your findings in the table.

Measure the length of every classmate's right arm in inches and in centimeters. Create a table to record your data. Design a query to sort the length in centimeters.

Using your most recent lab experiment, design a table listing the procedure, experiment, and results.

Design a table to list the capitals of the United States or the capitals of European or Asian countries. Also list the population of each capital city. Create a query to determine the cities with the largest and smallest populations.

Project 26

Gazing at the Stars

A **s a member** of your school's Star Gazers Club, you will be traveling in the United States this summer. You will travel one week each month and visit a different city in a different state. Since Star Gazers is an astronomy club, the main purpose of your trip is to view the constellations.

You will choose three cities and then use the Internet to research each city. Using database software, you will design a comparison table of information about each city. Using word processing software, you will compose a letter to the president of the Star Gazers that summarizes your findings.

Project Curriculum Skills

Language Arts, Social Studies, Mathematics, Science

In this project you will:

- ☑ **Locate three cities of interest in the United States**
- ☑ **Research specific data about each city**
- ☑ **Design a table**
- ☑ **Record data**
- ☑ **Insert new fields**
- ☑ **Determine the distance between cities**
- ☑ **Research the summer constellations**
- ☑ **Create a letter**

Locate Three Cities

1. Refer to the map of the United States in your classroom, if available.

2. Locate three cities that you would like to visit.

3. Jot down the names and states.

NOTE

Each city must be in a different state.

Design Your Table

1. Using database software, design a table that lets you compare your data easily.

2. Choose appropriate field names, as shown in Figure 26-1.

3. Save the table.

4. Keep the file open but minimize it.

NOTE

If you want to change a field name, you will be able to do so after the table is created.

City	State	Places of Interest	Accommodations	More Information (Phone/E-Mail)

Figure 26-1　Field names

Research Data about Each City

1. Go to *www.clickcity.com*. Bookmark this site.

2. Follow the directions to obtain information about each city.

3. Record the information in your table.

4. Save the table.

NOTE

If you need to revise a field name, you may do so.

Insert Two New Fields

1. Insert a field to record the distance in miles and kilometers from your hometown to each city.

2. Insert a field to record a constellation visible in June, July, and August in each city.

3. Save the table.

4. Keep the file open but minimize it.

NOTE

Use the Help feature of your software for steps on how to insert fields after a table is created.

Calculate Distance from City to City

1. Use an Internet search engine to search for map sites that provide driving directions.

2. Enter the starting address and destinations to calculate the mileage between cities.

3. Enter the mileage in your table.

4. Convert the miles to kilometers.

5. Save the table.

6. Keep the file open, but minimize it.

TIP

An easy-to-use site is *www.yahoo.com*. Click the link *Maps* and then *Driving Directions*.

Research and Record Constellations

1. Go to *www.clickcity.com*.

2. Type in the name and state of one of the cities you chose in Section 26-1.

3. Click **Weather**.

4. On the next Web page, click **Current Weather Conditions**.

5. Scroll down the page. Under **Features** click **Astronomy**.

6. In the **Fast Forecast** box, type in one city and state you chose.

7. On the next Web page, click **Astronomy**.

8. Select dates in June, July, and August and record a constellation for each month in your table.

9. Repeat step 8 for each city you chose.

10. Save the table.

NOTE

Remember that you are traveling to three cities on three dates. Don't forget to change your city in the forecast box before changing the date on the astronomy page.

Write a Letter

TIP

If available, use the letter wizard of your software.

TIP

Vary your vocabulary by using the thesaurus feature of your software.

TIP

Use the copy and paste features to copy the table into the letter.

1. Use your word processor to compose a letter to the president of Star Gazers, including your school's name and address. Use the correct format for writing a business letter.

2. Your letter should include the following.

   a. Introductory paragraph explaining the project

   b. Discussion of why you chose the cities you did

   c. Your table and a brief explanation of it

   d. Conclusion

3. Save the file.

Project 26

Curriculum Connection

Write a letter to the editor of your school newspaper about your recent study of constellations. Persuade the editor to include an astronomy section in each issue and offer to help gather the information.

Refer to the distances between cities that you listed in this project. Calculate how many hours it would take to drive from one city to the next at 60 miles per hour.

Make a table of the constellations visible in winter, spring, and fall in your hometown. Which constellations, if any, are present in two or more seasons?

Choose one of the cities you selected in this project. Use the Internet to gather in-depth information about the history of that city. Write an informative letter to the historical society of that city about your findings.

Project 27

Find the Cure!

You are working part-time at the middle school and have been asked to create a flyer about computer viruses. The flyer will be issued to all students and teachers to make them aware of common viruses and disinfecting procedures.

With a partner, you will research current viruses on the Internet and use the information you learn to create the flyer and a presentation for a schoolwide assembly.

In this project you will:

☑ **Do research on the Internet**

☑ **Create a flyer**

☑ **Create a presentation**

Project Curriculum Skills

Language Arts

Internet Research

1. Use a search engine to research current computer viruses. You may also want to try the following URLs: *http://csrc.ncsl.nist.gov/virus/*, *www.tju.edu/tju/dis/virus/*, *www.mcafee.com* (click **Free Virus News** at the bottom of the page), *www.zdnet.com/zdhelp/filters/splash/0,9700,6008986,00.html*, and *www.norton.com* (click **Security Updates**).

2. Use your word processor to record the following information. You will use this information in the flyer you'll create in Section 27-2.

   a. Definition of a computer virus

   b. Current viruses

   c. Common warning signs

   d. Cures for common viruses

   e. Virus myths and hoaxes

   f. Where to go for help

3. Save the file.

Flyer

1. Create a flyer for distribution to your school's students and staff. Use the information you gathered in Section 27-1 to create the flyer.

2. Be sure to cite your sources in the flyer.

3. Save the file.

TIP

A flyer should contain an attention-grabbing headline and use color and graphics. It should be clear and easy to read. Your flyer will be printed on regular 8½ by 11-inch paper.

Find the Cure!

Presentation

You have been asked to present your findings to the school during an assembly.

TIP

Practice your presentation ahead of time. Time yourself so that the presentation runs about 10 minutes.

1. Prepare a 10-minute presentation for the assembly.

2. Create a title slide and a slide for each of the six topics in the flyer.

3. Include graphic elements.

4. Be prepared to answer questions about computer viruses.

Curriculum Connection

Write a paragraph about computer virus prevention for students. How can students protect their computers at home?

Go online to explore the antivirus software packages that are available to consumers. Which are rated the highest by valid sources? How do their prices compare? Create a spreadsheet that lists five antivirus programs, their prices, and their ratings. Sort the list in order of best to worse.

Create a flyer for your school's science department. Use bullets to list courses available and other important information. Use the shapes tool to create colorful shapes to frame your text.

Think about the damage a virus can do to your own computer. Now consider the damage that could be inflicted on a corporation or government agency by viruses. Research the Michelangelo virus online. Using your word processing software, respond to the following questions. How is this virus activated? What does it do? How did this virus affect corporations, organizations, and individuals in the United States? Was the damage from this virus as serious as expected? Why or why not?

Part 4 Capstone Project

The Case of the E-Mail Enigma

The Case of the E-Mail Enigma

Project 28

VIRUS BUSTERS, INC.
Poised on the Edge

UCLA computer majors, Poindexter Chip and his best friend Norton Pixel, were determined to be millionaires before they turned thirty. They knew the most likely source of this fortune would be a computer-related company, since they both loved tinkering with computers and programs. The saga began in 1990, in Poindexter's dorm room, where his father had installed a state-of-the-art computer.

In this project you will:
- ☑ **Create a database**
- ☑ **Create a query**
- ☑ **Create spreadsheets**
- ☑ **Create a chart**
- ☑ **Write a report**
- ☑ **Prepare a presentation**

Project Curriculum Skills

Language Arts, Social Studies, Science, Mathematics

After their computer was infected with a nasty virus that crashed the system, Poindexter and Norton decided to make antivirus software and services their fledgling company's main products. For their graduation project, the pair developed antivirus software that effectively protected systems from all known viruses and could automatically adapt to protect against new viruses as they were discovered.

After graduation, Chip and Pixel formed their own company and called it Virus Busters. They worked 16-hour days and distributed flyers describing their services to local businesses. They offered their services free to get a "foot in the door." Soon, Virus Busters and Chip and Pixel became familiar names in the industry. However, with their increasing success came new pressures. Disagreements over company decisions became more frequent, and Chip and Pixel's friendship began to unravel. In 1992, Pixel left Virus Busters to form his own competing business.

Two years later, in 1994, Pixel's company went bankrupt, and he was offered a position as a software engineer at Virus Busters. Swallowing his pride, he accepted.

Today, Virus Busters' software is the top-selling antivirus product in the world, and its employees travel the globe disinfecting computer systems for industry and government. Poindexter Chip is a multimillionaire.

All is not well at Virus Busters, however. As the number one antivirus company in the world, Virus Busters is under pressure to develop an antidote for a deadly virus that is crashing computer systems worldwide. To make matters worse, on March 7 of this year, Virus Busters employee Vernon C. Byte was found dead in his office—strangled by his own mouse cord.

You and your partner in a detective agency are members of a special investigative team hired by the Silicon Valley Police Department. Your job is to find Byte's murderer.

Procedure

Your team will receive a file containing information gathered by police investigators. You may also use the information in Figure 28-1 and Figure 28-2 to solve the mystery. Your teacher will be your contact throughout the investigation. Each of you will need to give your teacher specific documents and reports. As you study the evidence, you will search for clues to the identity of Byte's murderer. Remember, in order to have backup copies of all data, each of you must create and save each file.

When your team has enough evidence (documented by databases, spreadsheets, and word processing documents) to accuse a specific suspect, each of you will prepare a word processing document. This document must contain your own theories and concrete evidence copied and pasted from other files to substantiate your accusation.

You must be extremely careful not to compromise the investigation by allowing leaks to the press. Do not disclose any evidence to other investigating teams.

Reimbursement

Keep track of the hours you spend on this case. You will be creating a spreadsheet from which to bill the police department.

Presentation

Finally, you will create a short slide show presentation of your conclusive evidence.

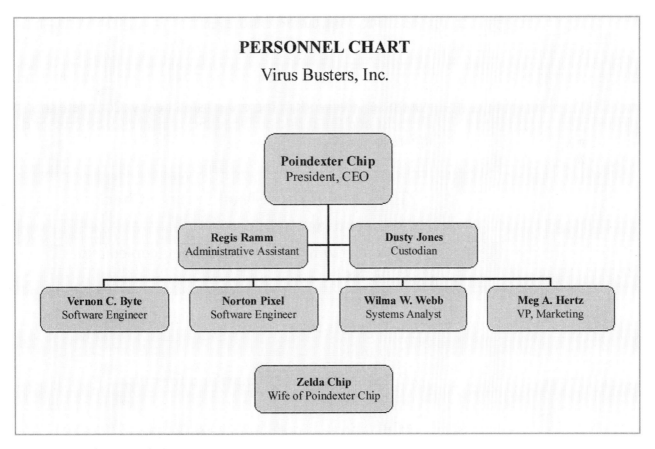

Figure 28-1　Personnel chart

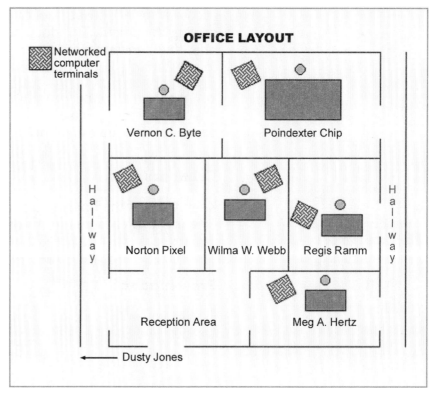

Figure 28-2   Virus Busters office layout

Assemble your work in the order listed below. Complete this checklist and the rubric provided by your teacher before handing in your work.

The Case of the E-Mail Enigma Checklist

☐ **Cover page**

☐ **Report with table/spreadsheet (copied and pasted)**

☐ **Crime information table**

☐ **Suspects table**

☐ **Query**

☐ **Spreadsheet with chart and formulas**

☐ **Pie chart**

☐ **Payroll spreadsheet with formulas**

☐ **Presentation slides**

Suspect Profiles

NOTE

These notes are for your own use and will not be collected.

NOTE

Each of you will have notes about all seven suspects in your word processing file.

TIP

Use the highlight formatting feature of your software.

Following is a list of the seven suspects and relevant information about them. At the end of this activity, you will have summarized significant information about each suspect.

1. Divide the reading of each profile between you and your partner.

2. Make notes in a word processing file on anything you think is significant or important.

3. Switch with your partner and read the remaining profiles.

4. Continue to make notes.

5. Compare notes with your partner.

6. Highlight important facts.

7. Save the file.

SUSPECT PROFILES

The investigative team of the Silicon Valley Police Department asked for background information on the employees of Virus Busters. The team then compiled this list of possible suspects in the murder.

Zelda Chip, Wife of Poindexter Chip, President and CEO

Poindexter and Zelda met in their junior year at UCLA in a computer programming class. At first they were friends and often worked together writing programs. In the spring of their senior year, they made a presentation together at a computer convention. When Zelda and Poindexter realized how strongly they felt about the configuration of motherboards, they fell madly in love. It seemed to be a match made in virtual heaven. After they graduated, Zelda went on to pursue her Master's degree in computer science. She now works as a programmer for CPUs Limited in San Francisco. She is very friendly with all the employees at Virus Busters. Zelda hosts many parties for the company's staff and has been nicknamed The Social Butterfly by the staff. Zelda's colleagues at CPUs Limited describe her as competitive and aggressive. Zelda owns 1,200 shares of stock in the company.

Wilma W. Webb, Systems Analyst

Wilma came to work for Virus Busters in 1992. She received her B.S. and M.S. degrees from Stanford University. Mr. Chip often talked about how impressed he was with her resume. Wilma's thesis for her Master's degree was *The Prolific Nature of Viruses*. She has told those close to her that stopping viruses is a lifelong hobby. Wilma has written, but never published, some software programs that can run on the Internet. She is single and very devoted to her work. Wilma is not assertive by nature; however, she aspires to be the CEO of her own company someday. Wilma owns 200 shares of stock in the company.

Regis Ramm, Administrative Assistant to Poindexter Chip

Regis has been Mr. Chip's "right-hand man" since the start of Virus Busters. Before this job he worked as a secretary in the Army for four years. Mr. Chip was impressed with his organizational skills and his self-motivation. Mr. Chip has been quoted as saying, "Regis is organized to a fault." Regis is not all business, however, and has been known to crack a joke or two on his breaks. He and Vernon always team up for a routine in the company's talent show. Regis's wife and three children get together socially with Vernon and his family. Regis seems happy in his job even though there has been no room for advancement. However, on occasion he has said such things as "Making more money would be nice" and "Who wouldn't like to be rich?" Regis owns 1,000 shares of stock in the company.

Dermot "Dusty" Jones, Custodian

Dermot "Dusty" Jones is the brother-in-law of Vernon C. Byte. Dusty works the night shift at Virus Busters because he needs the extra cash. Vernon, aware of Dusty's mounting bills, recommended him for the job. Dusty is a quiet, no-nonsense guy: You give him a job to do, and he does it. Vernon didn't have a close relationship with Dusty, and he felt that Dusty was hard to talk to. Dusty is also taking Saturday courses at the community college. His day job is assistant manager at the Home & Building Supply store. He never has time to do anything fun. The most fun he ever had was playing linebacker for his high school football team. Dusty owns no stock in the company.

Poindexter Chip, President and CEO

Poindexter is a cofounder of Virus Busters and since 1992 has held the reins in this prosperous company. He has a flamboyant, somewhat overbearing personality and clearly enjoys the spotlight. It is said that he would be nothing without the brains and talent of Norton Pixel. Chip runs the firm with an iron hand and is not well loved by his employees. Poindexter owns 2,000 shares of stock in the company.

Meg A. Hertz, VP, Marketing

Meg joined Virus Busters in 1995 after a rapid ascent of the corporate ladder at IoTech, Inc. She left IoTech in the midst of a scandal involving illegal stock trading. Although she was not prosecuted, it was whispered that she was a player in the illicit deals. She is known for her quick mind and brilliant marketing tactics. The six-foot tall Hertz works out at the gym every day during lunch. Meg owns 600 shares of stock in the company.

Norton Pixel, Software Engineer

Norton is a cofounder of Virus Busters and, some say, the true brains behind the organization. Although he seems to prefer to stay in the background, allowing the more colorful Poindexter Chip to garner the glory, it seems he must be somewhat resentful that he has not been promoted. Norton is unmarried and is totally committed to his work, often working far into the night. Norton owns 500 shares of stock in the company.

PROFILE OF VICTIM

Vernon C. Byte, Software Engineer

Vernon was the project leader in the search for an antidote to a deadly virus that is crashing computer systems throughout the world. He was known to spend 24 hours a day in his office in his quest. At a recent staff and stockholders meeting, Poindexter Chip promised any employee who averted the crisis 500 additional shares of stock. Vernon bragged about his potential good fortune at family gatherings, hinting that he was on the verge of perfecting an antidote for the virus. At the time of his death, he owned 500 shares of stock.

> **NOTE**
>
> Stock represents ownership in a company. The more stock an individual owns, the more control he or she has in the decision-making process, and the more money he or she will make when the company does well.

Time Spent on Task 60 minutes

Gathering Information

The Crime Notes that follow contain significant information relating to the crime. In this activity, you will organize this data in a database.

Person Reporting	Time Arrived at Scene	Fact 1	Fact 2	Fact 3

Figure 28-3   Crime notes table

1. Read the Crime Notes.

2. Open a new database file for the Crime Notes summary.

3. Create a new table.

4. Field names should be similar to those shown in Figure 28-3.

5. Save the table.

6. Enter data into the fields.

7. Save the table again.

CRIME NOTES

Police Officer Krupinski

At 9:15 p.m. I received a call from the custodian, Dusty Jones, at Virus Busters. He simply stated, "Vernon C. Byte, an employee, was murdered." I arrived at the company at approximately 9:45 p.m. Mr. Jones brought me to the scene of the crime. He seemed very businesslike and unemotional about what had just happened.

When I opened the door to Mr. Byte's office, I didn't see him at first. He was on the floor with the chair on top of him. I didn't touch the chair but bent down to get a look at him. There was no blood, but the mouse cord was wrapped tightly around his neck.

I immediately called the homicide team on my cell phone. I was then going to ask Mr. Jones to stand guard at the door, but he was nowhere to be found.

Homicide Investigator Buddy Brown

Mr. Byte was on the floor behind his desk, slumped underneath his chair. The mouse cord was tied tightly in a knot around his neck. The mouse was not attached to the computer. With a gloved hand, I hit a key on the keyboard to clear the screensaver. The screen showed Mr. Byte's e-mail message box. The open e-mail message was addressed to Mr. Poindexter Chip, but no message had been entered.

According to Dusty Jones, the door was closed and locked when he arrived to clean. A picture was overturned on the bookshelf. I picked it up with a gloved hand and saw that it was a picture of Mr. Byte's wife and two children.

I inspected his computer. His hard drive contained only seven routine files unrelated to this case. I looked in his desk and on his shelves for disks. There were no disks anywhere.

Everything else in the office looked undisturbed, however, a heavy-duty broom and dustpan were propped up in the far corner of the room.

Medical Examiner Dr. Anne T. Backteria

The cause of death was strangulation. Victim's body had multiple bruises on the neck. A bruise on the skull could have been caused by a blunt instrument. Victim may have become unconscious before being strangled. Death occurred between 8:45 and 9:00 p.m.

Police Forensics Report

The only fingerprints found in the office were those of Mr. Byte. The mouse and mouse cord were free of prints. The telephone on his desk showed some smudged prints and those of Mr. Byte. The broom and dustpan in the corner were also clean. All the keys on the keyboard showed the prints of Mr. Byte except the Delete key, which had been wiped clean.

Time Spent on Task 120 minutes

Suspect Interviews Database

Following are two sets of interviews with each suspect. Each interview contains vital information for solving the case.

In this activity, you will organize the key information from these interviews in a database.

NOTE

It is important that both you and your partner read the interviews.

1. Read the Scenario 1 or Scenario 2 interview assigned to you by your teacher.

2. Open a new database file.

3. Create a new table for the Suspect Interviews summary.

4. Field names should be similar to those shown in Figure 28-4.

First Name	Last Name	Position	Last time victim seen on March 7	Can alibi be confirmed?

Figure 28-4   Suspect interviews fields

5. Save the table.

6. Enter data into the fields.

7. Save the table again.

8. Create a query for suspects whose alibis *cannot* be confirmed.

9. Save the query.

SUSPECT INTERVIEWS: SCENARIO 1

Zelda Chip, Wife of CEO and President, Poindexter Chip

Describe your last contact with Vernon C. Byte.

I think it was two or three days before his death. I had stopped by the office to give Poindexter some research materials. I always make it a point to visit with everyone before I leave.

What was Vernon doing when you visited him?

Actually, he wasn't in his office. He was by the copy machine. He was short with me. He apologized and said that he had to get something done and mumbled something about running out of time.

What was your reaction to his abruptness?

I was a bit hurt, but I said, "Okay, talk to you later."

Do you recall the time of day that you were there and about how long you stayed?

It must have been after lunch because that week I had meetings every morning. I would guess it was around 2:00 p.m. I was there only about 30 minutes.

Where did you go after Virus Busters?

I went back to work.

Did you mention Vernon's unusual behavior to anyone, including your husband?

No, I did not.

Do you know Vernon's e-mail password?

Yes, but I assure you everyone at Virus Busters knows his password. He was foolishly trusting.

What was your personal relationship with Mr. Byte?

We were friendly. My husband and I socialized with him and his family at company outings and at our house. We socialized with all the employees and their families, however.

Where were you on March 7, between 8:30 p.m. and 10:00 p.m.?

I was home by myself.

Wilma W. Webb, Systems Analyst

Describe your last contact with Vernon C. Byte.

I guess it was around 4:30 p.m. on March 7.

Could you describe any conversation the two of you had at that time?

Well, I need to give you some background first. About a week before his murder, Vernon came to me very upset. He felt very strongly that a serious virus was about to strike computer systems internationally. He was working day and night trying to pinpoint the source of the virus. I offered my help. He gave me some specifics and I immediately went back to my office to work on the problem. You can never have too much help when you're trying to locate a deadly virus. So, on the afternoon of March 7, I stopped in to see Vernon before leaving. He looked horrible from lack of sleep.

How did Mr. Byte react when you offered your assistance?

He was very appreciative, of course. I have a lot of knowledge about viruses. Anyone in the field would eagerly accept my help.

When did you leave Virus Busters on March 7?

I left about 5:00 p.m.

What was your personal relationship with Mr. Byte?

We didn't have any. It was all business between us. When we were thrown together socially, we were polite with one another, but that's it.

Do you know Vernon's e-mail password?

A person's password is sacred. Why would I know that?

Where were you on March 7, between 8:30 p.m. and 10:00 p.m.?

I was at a computer club meeting in Santa Cruz. I didn't get home until 10:30 p.m.

Can you give me a list of the computer club's members so that we can confirm your whereabouts?

Yes. I will give you a list tomorrow.

Regis Ramm, Administrative Assistant to Poindexter Chip

When was the last time you saw Vernon C. Byte?

That would be 16:45 hours on Monday, March 7.

Could you translate that into regular hours, please?

Oh, yes, I'm sorry. That would be 4:45 p.m.

When did you leave Virus Busters on March 7?

It was about 8:00 p.m. I forgot my coat, went back down the hall, waved goodbye to Mr. Chip and Dusty, and left.

What was your working relationship with Mr. Byte?

Since I am Mr. Chip's assistant, anyone in the office has to go through me to see him. Anytime Vernon needed to schedule appointments with or speak to Mr. Chip, I would arrange it.

Would Mr. Byte ever call Mr. Chip directly?

I can't really say. I guess it's possible.

What was your personal relationship with Mr. Byte?

Vernon and I were close friends. I'm going to miss him greatly.

Could you elaborate on your social relationship?

Well, our families would get together at each other's house for dinner on a monthly basis. Vernon and I also had a comedy act in the company talent show. He and I would rehearse in my garage a couple times a week before the show. Vernon always liked a good joke.

Do you know Vernon's e-mail password?

Yes, I do. I am the e-mail administrator for all employees. All the employees have to log their passwords with me. However, I do not have these recorded on disk. I have a printout of them and they are locked in the company's safe.

Why do you need them printed out?

If there is ever a problem logging on to the e-mail service, the administrator might need to contact the provider and work out the problem.

As e-mail administrator, can you tell me who received an e-mail from Vernon on or around March 7?

Yes. Just let me access my computer for a second. Okay, here it is. Vernon sent e-mail only to Poindexter Chip, Wilma W. Webb, and Norton Pixel. That's it.

Can anyone else access that same e-mail information?

No, they would have to know the passwords in order to log in to that part of the server.

Where were you on March 7, between 8:30 p.m. and 10:00 p.m.?

I was home with my wife and kids.

Dermot "Dusty" Jones, Custodian

When was the last time you saw Vernon C. Byte?

Alive or dead?

When was the last time you saw him alive, please?

Guess it was March 6 at about 6:00 p.m.

Was it normal for Mr. Byte to be in his office at 6:00 p.m.? Did you usually see him when you reported for work?

Well, no, I usually didn't see him when I got to work. The last few weeks, though, he was there every night.

What are your hours at Virus Busters?

My hours are Monday through Friday from 5:30 p.m. to 9:30 p.m.

At what time did you discover the body of Mr. Byte?

It must have been around 9:00 p.m.

Was the door to his office locked?

Yes.

What were you going to do in his office?

Clean it.

Can you state for me the order in which you clean the offices at Virus Busters?

Okay. I start with Mr. Chip's. Then I clean the rest in this order: Ramm, Hertz, Webb, Pixel, and Byte.

So Mr. Byte's is the last office you clean each night?

Yeah, that's right.

About how long does it take you to clean each office?

About 15 minutes.

Now, let's go back to the night of March 7. Describe for me exactly what took place after you opened the door to his office.

Well, I turned on the light and wheeled in my cleaning cart. I immediately saw that his chair had been overturned. I walked around his desk and saw Vernon slumped underneath the chair. I called out his name. When he didn't respond, I called 911 from his phone.

You used Mr. Byte's phone, then, to call 911?
Yeah, that's right.

What did you do after you made the call?
I left the office. It was creepy in there, you know?

Where did you go?
I went down to the lobby to wait for the cops.

Did you leave your cleaning cart in the office?
No, I wheeled it back into the supply closet on that floor.

So, you didn't leave anything in the office?
No, not that I can remember.

Do you know Vernon's e-mail password?
What's a password?

How would you describe your personal relationship with Vernon Byte?
He was my brother-in-law. That's about it. We weren't close. He was such a computer geek. We had nothing in common. My wife didn't talk to him much either. You couldn't even talk to him about pro football!

Were you aware that Vernon's will left all of his stock to your wife?
No, I had no idea.

Did you leave at 9:30 p.m., your regular time, on the night of Mr. Byte's murder?
No, I hung around until the cops left. I guess it was around 10:30 or 11:00 p.m.

Poindexter Chip, President and CEO

Describe your last contact with Vernon C. Byte.
It was roughly 6:00 p.m. on March 7.

Did you discuss anything with Mr. Byte at that time?
Well, I had been quite concerned about Vernon's behavior about two weeks before his death. He was at work longer than usual and he seemed uptight—really stressed. I tried to get him to open up, but he just said, "I'll e-mail you as soon as I have something concrete."

So this behavior was not normal for Mr. Byte?

No, it was not. We could usually sit down and go over things at length. I had never seen him so driven.

When did you leave Virus Busters on March 7?

I left about 6:15 p.m.

Could you describe Mr. Byte's job duties in detail?

Well, as you know, Vernon was a software engineer. He wrote programs that prevent and erase viruses from systems. Vernon was a very valuable employee. He worked many hours and seemed to like his job very much.

Did you receive an e-mail from Mr. Byte on March 7?

No, I did not.

Do you know Mr. Byte's password?

Well, I don't, but I know my administrative assistant, Mr. Ramm, has all the employees' passwords locked up in the safe.

Did you ever socialize with Vernon?

Yes, my wife and I had many company parties at our home. Vernon and his family always attended.

Where were you on March 7, between 8:30 p.m. and 10:00 p.m.?

I was home with my wife.

Norton Pixel, Software Engineer

Describe your last contact with Vernon C. Byte.

I worked late on March 7 and poked my nose in his office around 7:00 p.m. to say good night.

What was Mr. Byte doing at that time?

He didn't even look up from his computer. He simply waved goodbye and sort of grunted at me. I closed his door and left.

When did you leave Virus Busters on March 7?

I left about 7:10 p.m.

What is your relationship with Vernon Byte?

He was already an established software engineer here when I joined the company the second time around. We worked on individual projects—we hardly ever worked together. We had very different ways of approaching a project.

Did you ever socialize with Mr. Byte?

No. We were two very different personalities. We were at company parties together, but we didn't talk even there.

Where were you on March 7 between 8:30 and 10:00 p.m.?

The Case of the E-Mail Enigma

I stopped at a restaurant for dinner and got home around 10:00 p.m.

What was the name of the restaurant?

The Internet Café. It's my favorite restaurant. I can surf the Net while I eat.

Do you know Vernon's e-mail password?

Yes, everybody knew his password. He asked people to check his mail for him.

Meg A. Hertz, VP, Marketing

Describe your last contact with Vernon C. Byte.

I saw him around 6:30 p.m. on March 7. I stopped in to say goodbye before I left.

Did you talk with him?

No, we just exchanged goodbyes and then I left.

What is your relationship with Mr. Byte?

I admire his brilliant work, but we had little in common, since my area is marketing, not computers. I saw him socially at company gatherings.

I understand that you left IoTech in the midst of a stock scandal. Was there a reason you left at that time?

It was pure coincidence that I chose to leave at that time. There was no conclusive evidence to suggest that I was involved.

Where were you on March 7 between 8:30 and 10:00 p.m.?

I went to the gym until about 8:00 p.m. and then window-shopped on Main Street. I got home about 10:30 p.m.

Did you talk with anyone in particular at the gym?

No, I never socialize there.

Do you know Vernon's e-mail password?

No, how would I know something like that?

SUSPECT INTERVIEWS: SCENARIO 2

Zelda Chip, Wife of CEO and President, Poindexter Chip

Describe your last contact with Vernon C. Byte.

I think it was two or three days before his death. I had stopped by the office to give Poindexter some research materials. I always make it a point to visit with everyone before I leave.

What was Vernon doing when you visited him?

Actually, he wasn't in his office. He was by the copy machine. He was short with me. He apologized and said that he had to get something done and mumbled something about running out of time.

What was your reaction to his abruptness?

I was a bit hurt, but I said, "Okay, talk to you later."

Do you recall the time of day that you were there and about how long you stayed?

It must have been after lunch because that week I had meetings every morning. I would guess it was around 2:00 p.m. I was there only about 30 minutes.

Where did you go after Virus Busters?

I went back to work.

Did you mention Vernon's unusual behavior to anyone, including your husband?

No, I did not.

Do you know Vernon's e-mail password?

Yes, but I assure you everyone at Virus Busters knows his password. He was foolishly trusting.

What was your personal relationship with Mr. Byte?

We were friendly. My husband and I socialized with him and his family at company outings and at our house. We socialized with all the employees and their families, however.

Where were you on March 7, between 8:30 p.m. and 10:00 p.m.?

I was home with my husband.

Wilma W. Webb, Systems Analyst

Describe your last contact with Vernon C. Byte.

I guess it was around 4:30 p.m. on March 7.

Could you describe any conversation the two of you had at that time?

Well, I need to give you some background first. About a week before his murder, Vernon came to me very upset. He felt very strongly that a serious virus was about to strike computer systems internationally. He was working day and night trying to pinpoint the source of the virus. I offered my help. He gave me some specifics and I immediately went back to my office to work on the problem. You can never have too much help when you're trying to locate a deadly virus. So, on the afternoon of March 7, I stopped in to see Vernon before leaving. He looked horrible from lack of sleep.

How did Mr. Byte react when you offered your assistance?

He was very appreciative, of course. I have a lot of knowledge about viruses. Anyone in the field would eagerly accept my help.

When did you leave Virus Busters on March 7?

I left about 5:00 p.m.

What was your personal relationship with Mr. Byte?

We didn't have any. It was all business between us. When we were thrown together socially, we were polite with one another, but that's it. The only person I socialize with from work is Meg. We collaborated on the virus problem. She was determined to win Poindexter's stock bonus in order to have more clout in the company.

Do you know Vernon's e-mail password?

A person's password is sacred. Why would I know that?

Where were you on March 7, between 8:30 p.m. and 10:00 p.m.?

I was at a computer club meeting in Santa Cruz. I didn't get home until 10:30 p.m.

Can you give me a list of the computer club's members so that we can confirm your whereabouts?

Yes. I will give you a list tomorrow.

Regis Ramm, Administrative Assistant to Poindexter Chip

When was the last time you saw Vernon C. Byte?

That would be 16:45 hours p.m. on Monday, March 7.

Could you translate that into regular hours, please?

Oh, yes, I'm sorry. That would be 4:45 p.m.

When did you leave Virus Busters on March 7?

It was about 8:00 p.m.

What was your working relationship with Mr. Byte?

Since I am Mr. Chip's assistant, anyone in the office has to go through me to see him. Anytime Vernon needed to schedule appointments with or speak to Mr. Chip, I would arrange it.

Would Mr. Byte ever call Mr. Chip directly?

I can't really say. I guess it's possible.

What was your personal relationship with Mr. Byte?

Vernon and I were close friends. I'm going to miss him greatly.

Could you elaborate on your social relationship?

Well, our families would get together at each other's house for dinner on a monthly basis. Vernon and I also had a comedy act in the company talent show. He and I would rehearse in my garage a couple times a week before the show. Vernon always liked a good joke.

Do you know Vernon's e-mail password?

Yes, I do. I am the e-mail administrator for all employees. All the employees have to log their passwords with me. However, I do not have these recorded on disk. I have a printout of them and they are locked in the company's safe.

Why do you need them printed out?

If there is ever a problem logging on to the e-mail service, the administrator might need to contact the provider and work out the problem.

As e-mail administrator, can you tell me who received an e-mail from Vernon on or around March 7?

Yes. Just let me access my computer for a second. Okay, here it is. Vernon sent e-mail only to Wilma W. Webb, Meg A. Hertz, and Norton Pixel. That's it.

Can anyone else access that same e-mail information?

No, they would have to know the passwords in order to log in to that part of the server.

Where were you on March 7, between 8:30 p.m. and 10:00 p.m.?

I was home with my wife and kids.

Dermot "Dusty" Jones, Custodian

When was the last time you saw Vernon C. Byte?

Alive or dead?

When was the last time you saw him alive, please?

Guess it was March 6 at about 6:00 p.m.

Was it normal for Mr. Byte to be in his office at 6:00 p.m.? Did you usually see him when you reported for work?

Well, no, I usually didn't see him when I got to work. The last few weeks, though, he was there every night.

What are your hours at Virus Busters?

My hours are Monday through Friday from 5:30 p.m. to 9:30 p.m.

At what time did you discover the body of Mr. Byte?

It must have been around 9:00 p.m.

Was the door to his office locked?

Yes.

What were you going to do in his office?

Clean it.

Can you state for me the order in which you clean the offices at Virus Busters?

Okay. I start with Mr. Chip's. Then I clean the rest in this order: Ramm, Hertz, Webb, Pixel, and Byte. No, wait—that night I had to go back to Hertz's office at the end, because someone was working in there at 8 o'clock when I got to her office.

So Mr. Byte's is the last office you clean each night?

Yeah, that's right.

About how long does it take you to clean each office?

About 15 minutes.

Now, let's go back to the night of March 7. Describe for me exactly what took place after you opened the door to his office.

Well, I turned on the light and wheeled in my cleaning cart. I immediately saw that his chair had been overturned. I walked around his desk and saw Vernon slumped underneath the chair. I called out his name. When he didn't respond, I called 911 from his phone.

You used Mr. Byte's phone, then, to call 911?

Yeah, that's right.

What did you do after you made the call?

I left the office. It was creepy in there, you know?

Where did you go?

I went down to the lobby to wait for the cops.

Did you leave your cleaning cart in the office?

No, I wheeled it back into the supply closet on that floor.

So, you didn't leave anything in the office?

No, not that I can remember.

Do you know Vernon's e-mail password?

What's a password?

How would you describe your personal relationship with Vernon Byte?

He was my brother-in-law. That's about it. We weren't close. He was such a computer geek. We had nothing in common.

My wife didn't talk to him much either. You couldn't even talk to him about pro football!

Were you aware that Vernon's will left all of his stock to your wife?

No, I had no idea.

Did you leave at 9:30 p.m., your regular time, on the night of Mr. Byte's murder?

No, I hung around until the cops left. I guess it was around 10:30 or 11:00 p.m.

Poindexter Chip, President and CEO

When was the last time you saw Vernon C. Byte?

It was roughly 6:00 p.m. on March 7.

Did you discuss anything with Mr. Byte at that time?

Well, I had been quite concerned about Vernon's behavior about two weeks before his death. He was at work longer than usual and he seemed uptight—really stressed. I tried to get him to open up, but he just said, "I'll e-mail you as soon as I have something concrete."

So this behavior was not normal for Mr. Byte?

No, it was not. We could usually sit down and go over things at length. I had never seen him so driven.

When did you leave Virus Busters on March 7?

I left about 6:15 p.m.

Could you describe Mr. Byte's job duties in detail?

Well, as you know, Vernon was a software engineer. He wrote programs that prevent and erase viruses from systems. He was a very valuable employee. He worked many hours and seemed to like his job very much.

Did you receive an e-mail from Mr. Byte on March 7?

No, I did not.

Do you know Mr. Byte's password?

Well, I don't, but I know my administrative assistant, Mr. Ramm, has all the employees' passwords locked up in the safe.

Did you ever socialize with Vernon?

Yes, my wife and I had many company parties at our home. Vernon and his family always attended.

Where were you on March 7, between 8:30 p.m. and 10:00 p.m.?

I was home with my wife.

Norton Pixel, Software Engineer

Describe your last contact with Vernon C. Byte.

I worked late on March 7 and poked my nose in his office around 7:00 p.m. to say good night.

What was Mr. Byte doing at that time?

He didn't even look up from his computer. He simply waved goodbye and sort of grunted at me. I closed his door and left.

When did you leave Virus Busters on March 7?

I left about 7:10 p.m.

What is your relationship with Vernon Byte?

He was already an established software engineer here when I joined the company the second time around. We worked on individual projects—we hardly ever worked together. We had very different ways of approaching a project.

Did you ever socialize with Mr. Byte?

No. We were two very different personalities. We were at company parties together, but we didn't talk even there. The only person from work I socialize with is Meg. We like to follow the stock market together. I'm always picking her brain about trading.

Where were you on March 7 between 8:30 and 10:00 p.m.?

I stopped at a restaurant for dinner and got home around 10:00 p.m.

What was the name of the restaurant?

The Internet Café. It's my favorite restaurant. I can surf the Net while I eat.

Do you know Vernon's e-mail password?

Yes, everybody knew his password. He asked people to check his mail for him.

Meg A. Hertz, VP, Marketing

Describe your last contact with Vernon C. Byte.

I saw him around 6:30 p.m. on March 7. I stopped in his office to say goodbye before I left.

Did you talk with him?

No, we just exchanged goodbyes and then I left.

Did you notice anyone else in the office as you were leaving?

Just Dusty Jones, the janitor.

What is your relationship with Mr. Byte?

I admire his brilliant work, but we had little in common, since my area is marketing, not computers. I saw him socially at company gatherings.

I understand that you left IoTech in the midst of a stock scandal. Was there a reason you left at that time?

It was pure coincidence that I chose to leave at that time. There was no conclusive evidence to suggest that I was involved.

Where were you on March 7 between 8:30 and 10:00 p.m.?

I went to the gym until about 8:00 p.m. and then window-shopped on Main Street. I got home about 10:30 p.m.

Did you talk with anyone in particular at the gym?

No, I never socialize there.

Do you know Vernon's e-mail password?

No, how would I know something like that?

Time Spent on Task 30 minutes

Payroll Spreadsheet

1. Create a spreadsheet listing the name of your team member, the number of hours worked, the dates worked, total hours worked, and total pay. Your hourly rate of pay is $35. Enter a formula to calculate total hours worked and total pay received. If a team member was absent, he or she should not receive pay for that time.

2. Save your spreadsheet. You'll add more data to the spreadsheet in Section 28-8.

Time Spent on Task 30 minutes

Stock Spreadsheet and Charts

1. Create a spreadsheet listing shares of stock owned by all employees and suspects, including the victim. Be sure to list each person's name, title, number of shares, and current market value.

2. Each share is currently worth $187.

3. Add a formula to compute the total dollar value of each person's stock.

4. Make a column that shows percentage of ownership. Use a formula to compute the percentage.

5. From the spreadsheet, create a chart listing the name of each stockholder and number of shares owned. Use a bar or column chart. Change the color or shading of the chart components. Insert the chart below the spreadsheet.

6. Create a pie chart showing each stockholder and the percentage of stock he or she owns.

7. Save your spreadsheet.

Time Spent on Task 40 minutes

28-6 *Word Processing Document—Identify the Murderer*

1. Use your word processor to write a report identifying the murderer. Support your information with facts from the transcripts, background profiles, and police reports.

2. Copy and paste relevant information from your databases and spreadsheets into the report. This report should include the following.

   a. Cover page with graphics.

   b. Several paragraphs detailing the reasons for your decision and the process used to arrive at that conclusion.

   c. Copied and pasted data from databases and spreadsheets. Include any that contain information pointing to the murderer.

3. Save your document.

Presentation

1. With your partner, prepare three to four slides using your presentation software. Include the following information.

   a. A title slide that includes the name of your detective agency and its logo.

   b. The identity of the murderer.

   c. The motive for the murder and methods used by the murderer.

   d. Print a condensed view of your slides in black and white.

2. Save your presentation.

Payroll Spreadsheet

1. Update and print the payroll spreadsheet in regular view and in formula view.

2. Save your spreadsheet.